JUST

BED!

For Gil

Good friends & wonderful memories are part of the AG's code - exemplified by our recent pilgrimage to Holland.

Best Wishes & Happy Landings

Eddie Wheeler
ex 150/214/97 Pff Sqdns. RAF.

12 May 1991

The Author—April 1941

JUST TO GET A BED!

EDDIE WHEELER D.F.C.

A Square One Publication

First published in 1990 by
Square One Publications
Sansome Place, Worcester WR1 1RU

ISBN 1 872017 20 7

Typeset by Wyvern Typesetting, Worcester
in Plantin 11/13

Printed by The Ipswich Book Co. Ltd.
England.

TO THE 55,573 BRAVE MEN
OF BOMBER COMMAND WHO DIED
IN WORLD WAR II

THE CASE FOR BOMBER COMMAND

The year 1990 sees the celebration of the fiftieth anniversary of the Battle of Britain which officially started on 26th June 1940 and concluded on October 13th. During that period 246 bomber aircraft were reported as lost on offensive operations directly concerned with the struggle. I have little faith that this figure includes many unfortunate aircraft which, although managing to reach these shores, failed to land safely. Such incidents, (far from rare) tended to get counted as accidents. A high proportion of the crews involved lost their lives.

After the Battle of Britain was won and Hitler's invasion plans were abandoned forever, 'Butch' Harris visited all Bomber Units and praised their flying personnel. I personally heard him declare, in his habitual forthright manner, that honours for the victory were shared equally by Bomber Command and Fighter Command. Churchill had no intention of excluding us when he made his famous broadcasts. The successful campaign against the invasion bases would undoubtedly receive official recognition. But none ever came. A proportion of the men of Bomber Command who lost their lives in attacking the Channel ports have their names recorded in Westminster Abbey. But the tally is not comprehensive.

By the 26th June 1940, Hitler's plans to invade Britain had reached an advanced stage. This was plainly evidenced by the massing of invasion barges along the nearby French coast. Channel ports automatically became prime targets. Night after night, our objectives were places like Ostend and Calais, all packed with barges. The Germans were always more than ready for us with their countless and formidable flak batteries. There was never an element of surprise in our favour.

We were briefed that our enemy hoped to deter us by skilful deployment of anti aircraft weapons. Inclusion of an abnormal proportion of tracer ammunition made their 20 mm calibre barrages extremely conspicuous and doubly threatening. The strategy was to cover target areas by an intense and continuous barrage of unaimed light flak. Shooting usually started well before any attackers were within range. Calais, for instance, seemed to have an especially fiery ceiling provided by endless tracer streams. A most apt description was 'like a giant incandescent waterfall laid on its side'.

Terrific damage was inflicted on those barges by resolute low level attacks. In post-war years the eminent historian, A. J. P. Taylor stated that on 11th September 1940 Hitler expressly postponed the date of the invasion to 24th September. This was in view of the losses sustained by the invasion barges. He goes on to assert that 'on the night of 13th September an especially successful bombing attack did enormous damage, sinking no fewer than eighty huge barges in the port of Ostend alone. On 17th September, Hitler postponed his invasion plans indefinitely, having realised, more clearly than Goering, that no longer could vast concentrations of barges, troops and military stores be maintained in the face of Bomber Command's devastating attacks' . . . 'Bomber Command had destroyed a great part of the shipping and war material on which the invasion depended'.

Incidentally, any mention of 'barges', seemed merely to conjure up visions of canal towpaths and patient horses pulling long narrow boats. Hardly important targets.

As a final comment, I quote from Page 77 of the 'British Army Review' of August 1976 which states:- 'Traditionally the comparison has been made in terms of British fighters against Germans fighters and bombers combined. For some reason our Bomber Command has usually been left out of the calculation. Bomber Command's strikes against the invasion fleet in the Channel ports were to play a major part in forcing a decision on the German Navy to disband their 'Sea Lion' forces. No one would wish to detract for one moment from the magnificent achievements of 'The Few' but history must be served. It does no service to the R.A.F. to preserve a myth which in fact conceals a very considerable military achievement in terms of organisation and logistic support that contributed quite as much to the success of the Battle of Britain as the heroism of the Spitfire and Hurrican pilots in the air.' End of quote.

It is undeniably true that our comparatively remote bomber stations were not so easily accessible to gentlemen of the press or to busy MP's and eminent V.I.P.'s. We suffered as a consequence. Fighter Command enjoyed a much better 'lobby' by reason of proximity to the seats of power and influence, coupled with far more civilised 'visiting hours'. The result was a higher degree of fraternisation with far better photographic cover. And a lasting image.

SQN. LDR. G. HAWORTH, DFC, DFM, (Ret.), A.C.A. No. 1997

PART I

ONE

In the Beginning

It was surely fate that destined my entry into this World on 5th November 1920—a date traditionally celebrated as Guy Fawkes Day following the Gunpowder Plot to blow up the Houses of Parliament in 1605. The event was marked over the years by bonfires, fireworks and the burning of guys. Twenty years later, I too was to be involved realistically and dangerously with fires, explosives and the burning of my fellow men.

My father was a Fitter, luckily in regular employment but poorly paid in the poverty which seemed normal to us then. Home was a three-roomed tenement in the North London Borough of Islington. I had been preceded by two brothers, Fred and George, and was to be succeeded by another brother and two sisters, Harry, Doris and Maureen. There was no doubt that the accommodation was totally inadequate for a family of that size, but sleeping three to a bed was considered acceptable in the dominantly poorer families of that time. To feed and clothe this size of family was very difficult and consequently my mother had to supplement father's meagre income by taking part-time work as and when available, be it cleaning, laundering or whatever, one could not be selective but just grateful if such opportunities arose. Large families were the norm, and pregnancies were generally dreaded as they meant more mouths to feed and bodies to clothe, a constant nightmare to many parents in those days.

Given these circumstances, my mother was grateful to unload any of her 'chicks', and as a baby I was placed on the transfer list and found myself before the age of three in the hands of neighbours—a childless couple, Nan and George Routh, without the formalities of adoption. Of the six children, it was strange that I was to be the one singled out to leave my parents, but no doubt fate played its part again as I obviously gained from the loving care lavished on me by my 'adopted' parents, even if their resources too were meagre. The love and encouragement they gave me will always remain in my memory. Their part in the forming of my character was significant, and whereas my own father was negative in his attitude to my future education etc., George was always urging me to study and 'make something of myself'.

My early days at York Road (Islington) Junior School are a happy memory although discipline was very strict indeed. Even minor misdemeanours were punished strongly, canings abounded and confinements after school were a regular practice. We certainly learned to respect authority and if we complained to our parents or guardians concerning punishment at school we invariably got short shrift—and sometimes further pain for our trouble! So, unlike today, we were always in awe of our teachers, sometimes frightened by the disciplines, but I am sure we are better persons today as a result of it. Policemen too, came into the same category, hard but always scrupulously fair.

It was generally accepted that schooling would start at the age of six and continue to the age of 14 when one would hopefully expect to enter employment for a few shillings a week. School ran from 9 a.m. to 4.30 p.m. daily but there were no such things as school meals. We took our own sandwiches, which were invariably bread and dripping or jam, which were most unpalatable after being jammed into short-trouser pockets for hours. The one concession we enjoyed was one-third of a pint of milk a day, free of charge.

Emphasis was placed on learning arithmetic, English, handwriting and spelling—all of which I enjoyed thoroughly. It was all a far cry from the way things are done today.

I made good progress at Elementary School, achieving placings in the top three of 45 pupils in class which promptly earned me the reputation of 'creep' from my fellow pupils.

Outside school, we were always adventurous and looking for new challenges, the riskier the better. Swimming was learned the hard way. At the age of nine we were marched to the local baths at Caledonian Road and after undressing we lined up at the edge of the swimming bath. Those ready first would be at the shallow end, with the poor unfortunates who undressed last at the deep end. Invariably, I lined up last of all at the deep end due to the fact that I had to climb out of the dreaded combinations, a piece of all-in-one underwear which covered from shoulder to just above the knee. The teacher, a crippled Mr. Crossley would then shout "At the count of three you all jump in," whether you could swim or not. Of course, all those at the shallow end would jump in without hesitation but the rest would still be swinging their arms, preparing to jump but never able to find the courage. Crossley would then move along the line brandishing his stick and we had to decide which was the lesser of the two evils. I recall being petrified, but after a couple of whackings I would close my eyes and jump to find myself floundering out of my depth and swallowing mouthfuls of water. On swimming days I pleaded to be allowed to discard my combinations so that I could line up nearer the shallow end. After several sessions of this torment, during which time I had been 'rescued' repeatedly by the bath attendant, I found that I could do a dog-paddle and survive on my own. Eventually I developed into a useful swimmer, but it was a hard way to learn!

When we were ten years old, several of us would go to the Regents Park Canal which was forbidden for swimming, constantly evading the Police to swim almost daily. One day, my friend Johnny Hankin got into difficulties and we had to run for the Policeman whom we had been repeatedly dodging. Johnny was brought out but too late, he had died from drowning. That was the last of that venture and we turned to other activities.

Following publicity on a record attempt to scale Mount Everest, we decided we wanted to be climbers and we made foolhardy attempts to climb on to the 100 ft high roof of the School, and a glass covered roof of the King's Cross Potato Market. These affrays also met with disaster. One lad fell and was impaled on the school railings, another fell through the glass roof of the Potato Market and was killed. The next target was to climb on to the roof of York Road Tube Station, by hand-over-hand ascent on protruding bricks. On that occasion, disaster was only averted by the timely intervention of the fire brigade.

We may have been foolish young people then, but I think it proved our generation to be bold and fearless, which was to stand the country in good stead in the years to come.

We didn't have much to eat, our clothes were mainly second-hand or restored, our shoes were constantly holed and put back into use with the aid of cardboard inserts, but we were never miserable and enjoyed life as it came. We walked miles during the school holidays, never having the fare to ride on trams. Occasionally we would steal rides and get cuffed by the Conductors for our cheek. The tall white mansions adjacent to Regents Park were a target where we knew we could steal a pint or two of milk. Another ploy was for a gang of us to enter bakers' shops giving the impression that we were going to buy, whilst two lads at the back were taking cakes out of the window—enough to feed us all. Many's the time we were chased by irate shopkeepers. The Covent Garden fruit market always provided our free fruit requirements.

From the age of ten to 14 I was very keen on football and joined a local team called 'White Heather'—seeing myself destined for fame as an outside right. This meant training on the shingle pitches of the Recreation Ground at Brecknock where we perpetually picked up abrasions and bruising in the crunching tackles on the lethal surface. Match days on Saturday and Sunday mornings meant walking from Islington to the cinder pitches at Finsbury Park but we were always encouraged by the attendance of 'scouts' from the famous professional clubs like Arsenal, Spurs and West Ham, and fancied that one day we would be gracing the turf at either Highbury or White Hart Lane. On Saturday afternoons we would walk to either Arsenal or Spurs Football grounds to see our idols display their magnificent talents. Alex James, Dixie Dean, George Hunt and Cliff Bastin quickly became our favourites. The entrance fee to stand was one shilling (5p) but an arrangement was soon established whereby we would pay the attendant the shilling but three of us would crawl under the turnstile which of course would not register the entry. The attendant was happy with his profit and it had cost us only fourpence (2p) each. Capacity crowds of 60,000 and over were the norm for each first class match. The support for each team was vociferous and friendly banter between rival supporters was enjoyable but I very rarely experienced any violence or the mindless chanting so prevalent today. In the packed grounds it was common for us youngsters to be rolled down over the heads of the crowd so that we could have a safe view from the side of the pitch.

Academically, I was making good progress at Junior School and at the age of 11 we were informed that one free scholarship was being offered to the school, the lucky individual to attend Highbury County Secondary School. To the dismay of my school chums I achieved the highest examination marks and at Assembly before the whole school it was announced that I had been awarded the scholarship.

Attendance at the High School was subject to my parents' agreement that I would attend there until I was 16. My 'adopted' parents could not sign the agreement, my father refused to sign—voicing the opinion that I should go out to work when I was 14—"What had been good enough for me should be good enough for you!"

After long deliberations, the Education Authority finally accepted the signature of my 'Guardians' and so I embarked on my higher education.

My unhappiness started when I found that I was the only pupil not in possession of school uniform and immediately I became the 'odd one out'. A further embarrassment was that all pupils other than those living locally attended school dinners, and whilst I lived too far away to go home, my Guardians could not afford to pay for school meals. Faced with ridicule by other members of the school, I went into Highbury Park in all weathers on my own to eat my sandwiches away from prying eyes and the constant mental cruelty of which children can be so guilty. The vast majority of the pupils were Jewish from the Stamford Hill area, and whilst I was not and never have been anti-Semitic, they did play havoc with my life at that school, culminating one day in a confrontation with a classic bully-boy who found great delight in smashing my thermos flask which had been ill-afforded by my Guardians. This stupid act enraged me and I struck out at him and was engaged in a bloody fight surrounded by dozens of chanting kids until separated by a Form Master, who ruled that I was the instigator and punished me accordingly.

I think my mental attitude affected my physical health and alas, my attendance suffered with consequent under-achievement in exams. Life was pretty miserable at that stage and on reaching the ripe old age of 14 I decided that I wished to leave school, which was not easy in the light of the signed agreement to stay until I was 16. However, after many appeals my release was granted.

TWO

To Work

So, in 1934 I was to start my working life, but employment was not easy to come by. Lady Luck smiled on me and I was engaged as an Office Boy by Herbert & Sons Limited in Goswell Road, London, at a wage of 12s. 0d. (60p) a week for 48 hours including Saturday mornings, with no payment for overtime, and a promise that repetition of lateness of two minutes or more daily would result in loss of job without notice. Many times I sweated and panted as I ran the three miles to work to beat the two-minute deadline. The Office Manager, Mr. Stan Kitchen, a man probably in his mid-20s, gave me great encouragement and was to prove a life-long friend.

Of the 'princely' weekly wage I felt obliged to hand over 11s. 0d. (55p) to my very needy guardians, keeping 1s. 0d. (5p) for the available luxuries of the day—mostly a trip to the Cinema, and committing myself to the purchase of a cycle from Graves of Sheffield at 2s. 0d. (10p) per month.

Little did I think that I would be associated with Herbert & Sons Limited over the next 50 years, but much was to happen to me in the interim.

My concern now was that I was getting taller and outgrowing my fold-up bed located in the tiny kitchen at home, and this became more of a problem as time went on, when I began to get troublesome bouts of cramp.

In 1937/38 it was becoming evident that Adolf Hitler was

intent on annexing territories adjacent to the Reich and the storm clouds over Europe were massing.

At the Cinema one evening I saw George Formby in 'Something in the Air', and immediately I felt convinced that my salvation could lie in joining the R.A.F.—if only to get a bed large enough to accommodate me without doubling my knees with cramp!

For weeks I tossed and turned in my mouse-trap of a bed, considering all the pros and cons of joining up, what trade I could reasonably apply for, how I would adapt to training, but most of all dreading the fact of announcing my intentions of leaving home when Nan and George had been so loving and supportive and wondering how upset they would be after my departure.

From the time in 1909 when Bleriot had made the first air crossing of the English Channel, progress in powered flight had been phenomenal and in the comparatively short space of only 30 years, we had been thrilled by legendary names like Charles Lindbergh, Commander Kingsford-Smith, Amy Johnson, Wiley Post, Jim Mollison and Amelia Earhart.

In my short lifetime I had read with avid interest and had marvelled at the heroism of the men and women who had actually flown the Atlantic and had spanned the continents to Australia and South Africa in frail aircraft, the like of which today we would hesitate to fly round a circuit of an airfield. Those courageous flyers were an inspiration to us all in years to come.

The war-clouds were becoming more dominant in early 1939, newspapers were announcing recruitment campaigns for the armed services but Prime Minister Neville Chamberlain was telling everybody that there would be 'peace in our time'.

A further bout of cramp convinced me that I should make my move and I ventured to Ad Astral House in Kingsway, announced that I was 18 years old and sought a career with the R.A.F. The Recruiting Officer said that there were vacancies for Wireless Operators on a 6-year engagement and that subject to satisfactory medical examination and agreement by my legal parents I could be considered as an entrant to the General Duties Branch.

Rather than cause upset to my Guardians, I approached my father and mother, asking their permission to join the service. My father's reaction was negative—he didn't want to be involved. A plea to my mother, aware of my domestic problem, resulted in her accompanying me one Saturday morning to Kingsway in the April of 1939. After her assurance to the Recruiting Officer that she would authorise my entry to the R.A.F., I was taken to the Medical Examiner and underwent a rigorous examination. Having undergone the many tests—with the embarrassment of being stripped naked in the presence of other applicants for the first time in my life, I came to the final exercise of supplying a urine sample. My excitement was so intense that I just could not pass water in spite of listening to many running taps which apparently always did produce the goods. But not for me!—A quick trip to the local J. Lyons Corner House at Holborn to down two cups of coffee, then back to Ad Astral House—but still with no results. The Centre closed at midday for the weekend, so I was told to return on Monday morning to perform the final act.

Waking on Monday morning I decided not to pass water until I reached the Recruiting Centre and after much drinking of tea—imagine my agony having to wait to provide that sample! Finally, I filled three bottles and was harangued by the Medical Orderly who swore I was providing samples for the 20 applicants attending that morning.

Thinking my medical clearance paved the way for entry was another mistake! An aptitude test followed but by this time I knew how not to put square blocks into round holes—so I passed the second stage.

It was only then, when my Mother was asked to produce my birth certificate that I discovered my surname was not Wheeler. What a shock when you find that you are a SCHEIDWEILER with a German heritage and a great grandfather from Hanover. Even the R.A.F. Flight Lieutenant was somewhat taken aback at this revelation and after furtive glances and discussions in a back room with other Officers, it was decided to visit Somerset House in Aldwych to trace the family tree. Somewhat bemused by all this, I sat in awe in Somerset House whilst the investigations were proceeding. Later I was told that I would be accepted but that during my R.A.F. career I would be known as Edwin Scheidweiler—*alias* Wheeler.

My mother, née Dorothy Seymour Thompson, was of Irish descent and with the combination of my Father's German ancestry I imagined that the R.A.F. had strong reservations about my entry.

A period of waiting followed, until I was called to be attested at Uxbridge, Middlesex, and I was in a dilemma as to when I should tell Nan and George of my impending departure.

Within days of my R.A.F. medical, I contracted rheumatism in the knee and was crippled so badly that I could not move out of bed for days. I dreaded the possibility of receiving my call-up papers for early reporting, being unable to comply due to my current disability with possible consequent rejection on medical grounds. On 30th May 1939, still suffering considerable pain, Nan brought me the envelope bearing O.H.M.S. with a quizzical look and it was at that moment I knew I had ducked my responsibility to let her know that I had made a decision to leave home and for what reason? Before opening the envelope I said to Nan, "Please sit down, I have something to tell you which I sincerely hope you will understand." For 15 years I had received the love and devotion of Nan and George who had deprived themselves of so much to provide for me, so much generosity and character-making which I felt I could never repay. However, I had reached an important stage of my life, I was not content to be a cost clerk for ever and a day, and had decided to undertake a career in wireless telegraphy—and the best medium for this was the R.A.F. No mention of my domestic discomfort and that bloody awful collapsible iron bed-chair!! Nan would have been so terribly upset if she'd thought that she had been deficient in any way and I couldn't bear the thought of hurting such a lovable person. A few tears and then she said, "When will you be going?" I said "Probably in a month or so—these papers will confirm" Opening the envelope with trepidation and with Nan shaking, I read: "You have been accepted on a 6 year engagement etc. etc. Please report to Uxbridge R.A.F. station on 7th June 1939."—just one week away! Having broken the news to Nan and George, perhaps the seven days notice was best in the circumstances and alleviated the possibility of further distress of a longer waiting period. But my present physical condition worried me, should I ask for a deferment until I was fit again? The nagging feeling that I might be totally rejected if I revealed that I had acute rheumatism swayed me against this course of action. Come what may, I would report as directed.

By the morning of the 7th June my condition hadn't really improved, and the thought of saying goodbye was hardly relished. It had been bad enough saying my farewells to my colleagues at Herbert & Sons Ltd. where I had spent an enjoyable four years. In all, I felt pretty miserable venturing into the unknown. When the time came to be off, there were tears from both Nan and George who repeatedly said, "Take care of yourself son—don't forget us, please write often." Nan pushed a small packet into my hand and with tear-filled eyes I went, not bearing to look back until I reached the corner and gave a final wave.

As I walked to Kings Cross Station, I opened the brown paper packet to reveal an Ingersoll wristwatch—no accompanying message. The watch said it all. I had never before owned a watch—a luxury not enjoyed by many, it was something I knew they could ill-afford—and I treasured it for years to come.

PART II

THREE

A New Bed

Two days at Uxbridge for attestation, registration as an AC2 (Aircraftman Second Class) Number 647193, meeting other 'sprogs' from all walks of life and from distant parts of the U.K., and then clad in civvies with our little pieces of baggage ranging from brown paper parcels to carrier bags and the odd suitcase, we embarked on coaches for Cardington, Beds. to undertake an eight-week drill training course. This prospect appalled me for I was still suffering abominably from the vastly swollen rheumatic knee. We were allocated to our dormitory type huts for the period of the course and introductions were made to our fellow hutmates. I selected my bed in the middle of the dormitory and viewed it with the utmost delight, it was wide and long and would provide me, hopefully, with cramp-free hours for weeks to come. However, the R.A.F. did have my commitment for the next six years as part of the deal. Then, dental inspections, followed by vaccinations and innoculations were the order of the day. Uniform kitting out was delayed due to a shortage of supply so for the first week we remained in our civvies. Of course everybody looked forward to being in uniform—little knowing that we were destined to be in such outfit for the next six years.

For a lad who had hardly ever ventured out of Islington, Cardington was awe-inspiring. The huge airship hangars which had housed the R100 and R101 airships dominated the skyline. Memories were revived of the dirigibles flying over London, including the Graf Zeppelin and the R100/R101. The tragedy at Beauvais in Northern France where the R101 crashed on its way to India with a notable passenger list, seemed to mark the end of that mode of air transport.

The influx of recruits to Cardington seemed enormous, no doubt due to the urgency being expressed for bringing our armed services up to strength to meet the threat from Nazi Germany. Strange really how the recruits mostly in their teens became excited at the possibility of war—but generally accepting that Neville Chamberlain would pursue his Appeasement policy and allow Adolf Hitler to achieve his 'liebensraum' objectives without British involvement.

Within 48 hours, under the direction of a P.T.I. Instructor —Cpl. Sumpter, we were initiated into the art of making our beds, polishing the floors to a state where you could almost see in the reflection the colour of your eyes, painting white lines everywhere, black-leading the stove and pipes to the highest degree of polish, even polishing the inside of dustbins! Up at 6.30 am, ablutions, and to breakfast at 8 am. There followed an F.F.I. (Free from infection) inspection in the hut which entailed stripping completely naked and standing in front of your bed—sometimes for up to an hour—before the entry of the Medical Officer, sometimes a W.A.A.F., (Womens Auxiliary Air Force) who would give a cursory glance and march out. The waiting time for inspection gave rise to some hilarity since the occupants had time to make comparisons and comment on the different shapes and sizes of the genital organs on display. On occasions when hut members could not contain or conceal their mirth, this brought displeasure on the part of Cpl. Sumpter and prompted extra fatigue duties or cancellation of weekend furlough passes.

After a week we were detailed to report to the Equipment Section for kitting-out and this too proved to be a complete joke, in spite of the announced attendance of a tailor who would alter uniforms to suit our own distorted bodies. The procedure for issue was conducted by a Sergeant who from his visual assessment would decide what size you were. No tape measures were in sight and the only measurements asked of us were shirt collar and boot sizes. All else was at the Sergeant's discretion. We were flung the various items of clothing with a promise that any apparel vastly under or over-sized would be changed the following week. The kitting out for each person lasted only 20 minutes!

Back at the billet, it was like something out of Music Hall and chaps were writhing on the floor in great fits of laughter as the various misfits paraded around in their new apparel. *Short* underpants (3) could be found to accommodate the body from knee to over the shoulders. Tunics of the dog-collar variety invariably drooped off the shoulders, sleeves fit to suit an orang-utang, and necks when secured made the wearer look as if he would choke to death. Forage caps looked either like pimples or swamped the heads, resting safely on the ears.

We finally paraded for inspection by Cpl. Sumpter and the giggles still could not be muffled. Some men had to wear items of their civilian clothing to supplement the issued uniform because it was impossible to get into either the tunic or trousers. Baggy trousers, or trousers too short made up a hysterical group. However, the 'Tailor' would put things right we were assured, but for days afterwards we could not look at each other without bursting into tears of laughter. How we yearned again for our civvies!

The serious part of our drill training began, four hours in the morning and four in the afternoon. The first day saw me in agony and several times I thought I would faint from the pain in my rheumatic knee as we were ordered to "lift those knees, pound the ground with the feet, march and countermarch!" After each session I would return to the hut, collapse on the bed wreathed in sweat, dreading going out for the next session. After a week, I had penetrated the pain barrier. Suddenly I was aware of a fitness I'd never experienced before, and it was exhilarating.

Having never been introduced to the 'evils' of alcohol, my leisure time was restricted to evenings in the N.A.A.F.I. where tea and a 'wad' (bun) cost the princely sum of 2d. (1p). Pay as an AC2 was 2/– (10p) a day payable fortnightly out of which I made an allotment to Nan of 10/– (50p) a week and so had a residue of 8/– (40p) fortnightly less sixpence (2½p) a week contribution to the R.A.F. Association, I think—for the benefit of Widows and Orphans. One could never contemplate becoming very rich on 3/6 (18p) a week! I ventured to the N.A.A.F.I. Canteen most evenings for company and listened to some superb piano playing by one of the young recruits.

Once proficient with the skills of marching—encouraged by the constant bawling of P.T.I. (Physical Training Instructor) Corporals—we were issued with rifles and bayonets for rifle drill. This had its moments in that on many occasions bayonets were not fixed properly and on the order "slope arms", wicked 12-inch steels would fly into the air with a mad scramble to take avoiding action following. Drill instructors would go blue with rage at the chaos ensuing when the squads were already on the move before the order to "slope arms" was given. Our thoughts were that this was a bloody dangerous life, emphasised by the news that the C.O. (Commanding Officer) had walked into the propellor of a light aircraft and been decapitated.

After six weeks we were finally declared proficient and told that we were moving on to the No. 2 Electrical & Wireless School based at Yatesbury in Wiltshire for a 12-month course as trainee Wireless Operators. On 21st July 1939 we arrived at Yatesbury—a huge camp with hutted accommodation, about five miles from Calne.

After acclimatisation, we were introduced to our Wireless Instructors—mostly all civilians. My training was to be conducted by a Mr. Tommy Tickle who was an excellent character, full of humour. He told us that we would be trained in the manipulation of R/T and W/T Service Radios, fault finding, and that we would be required to send and receive Morse Code at 18 to 25 words per minute. With any luck we might make the grade after 12 months. Of the eight hours daily working, something like three hours was spent on receiving and sending Morse and we reached the point that 'di-di-dah-dit' ruled our lives.

FOUR

And Now to War

During August, Hitler was making all the noises and Poland was obviously under threat but we still could not imagine that Britain would become involved. Alas, on 1st September Poland was invaded and under the guarantees made by the U.K. Government to Poland it was evident that a showdown had arrived. We now listened to the radio bulletins constantly and when we heard that an ultimatum had been given to Germany to "withdraw from Poland by 11 am on Sunday 3rd September or a state of war would exist between our two countries"—we realised that there would be no going back and that the dreaded conflict was almost upon us. The whole camp was assembled on the square on Sunday morning 3rd September to await the radio broadcast by the Prime Minister. 11 am came and went, there was much speculation amongst the gathered assembly and finally Neville Chamberlain was heard to say that: "As no response had been received from the German Chancellor to the ultimatum that all German troops be withdrawn from Poland, a state of war now exists between our two countries".

The Commanding Officer then addressed us and said that as we were now at war, we were subject to the rules of war, and penalties for indiscipline, treason etc. were extremely severe, and that we were all to do our part to the utmost of our ability in execution of our duty to the nation.

Although Sunday was viewed as a normal day of rest, we would all be involved until the hours of darkness in the filling of sandbags and steps necessary to ensure the security of the station. On the following Tuesday, all Wireless Operator trainees were instructed to report to the Medical Section in groups of 12 at intervals of one hour and rumours were rife that we were being prepared for overseas duty. The full medical inspections were carried out over a number of days and included 'blowing the mercury' to test lung capacity. One had to blow the mercury to a desired level and hold it there for at least a full minute. One could never gauge the time but I remember collapsing after having held it at over two minutes—thank goodness I never smoked cigarettes at that time. After completion of exhaustive tests we were informed that we had been passed 'fit for aircrew duties' and it was our duty to volunteer for such. It was then that I realised the full Service meaning of 'Volunteer'. Those of us who had no desire to fly were cajoled, coerced or whatever, but the percentage of remustering to aircrew was very high. I remember saying ". . . My mum doesn't want me to fly and I agree with her totally!"

Our training was to be speeded up and whereas Morse speeds of 18—25 w.p.m. were originally required, this was reduced to 12 w.p.m. to ensure more passes—and consequently more aircrew recruits!

The 'phoney' war had set in and there was very little air activity apart from isolated raids on German shipping and port installations. It all seemed so 'gentlemanly'—no indiscriminate bombing of civilian populations or cities—how long could this last?

At Yatesbury we had our first taste of flying—in Dragon Rapides—six trainees at a time to undertake W/T (Wireless Telegraphy) air exercises transmitting and receiving basic messages. For the first three trips, most of us were occupied with being air-sick, and the tuning of the set and transmissions became secondary. Bouncing across the grass field, we had visions of what was to come in the weeks and months ahead and we were far from happy.

At this time also, there were scares that the I.R.A. (Irish Republican Army) would attempt acts of sabotage on military establishments in Britain and we were all to be on the alert. A water tower which supplied the camp was located on a hill surrounded by trees on the other side of the main road to Calne and was viewed as a potential target for saboteurs, hence the necessity to mount a guard throughout 24 hours daily. My turn for guard duty on the water tower arrived and the weather was foul, bucketing with rain, and I was assigned for night duty from 6 pm to 6 am next morning. The shifts were two hours on and two hours off, the rest period to be spent in a tent adjacent to the water tower. In reaching the site we had already become drenched. Our Lee Enfield .303 rifles were issued by the Sergeant of the Guard—and we saw live ammunition for the first time. Two guards were to patrol round the tower, meeting each other at about 10 minute intervals. The usual challenge procedures were outlined by the Sergeant. On approach to the tower, persons were to be challenged "Who goes there, friend or foe?"—if no response, the challenge once again. After the second challenge, if no reply, then to fire! Patrolling at night in pouring rain, surrounded by trees, was the most soul-destroying job imaginable. The boredom was suddenly broken by a distinct rustling in the trees. Petrified, I am sure my challenge "Who goes there?" was but a whisper. Further noises emanated from the trees—could be two or three assailants—but still no response to my next hysterical challenge. Panic stricken at the thought of the tower being attacked during my patrol, I released the safety catch on my rifle, aimed at the area from whence the distinct noises came and fired. There was a thump within the trees and my heart sank—"God, I've killed someone!" The sound of the shot brought the other Guard and the Sergeant running with shouts of "Bloody hell, what was that?" Shaking like a leaf, I was rooted to the spot whilst the Sergeant investigated. He returned with the news that I had shot a local farmer's cow which had strayed into the trees. Needless to say, I was not considered to be fit for further guard duty that night. I thought 'If that's how I re-acted tonight, what would I be like in the event of being a member of aircrew in action!'

In February 1940 our course on initial wireless training was curtailed and we were presented with our 'Sparks' badges and told that we were deemed to be Wireless Operators—to which Tommy Tickle said "God help you—and us!" Attention then focused on the Notice Board where lists of postings were published. I saw that I was to be attached to 11 Group Fighter Command at Duxford near Cambridge, as an R/T Cabin Operator in the Operations Room directing pilots of No. 19 Squadron against enemy activity within their sector. Most of the activity at that time was routine patrol and training but I found the work most enjoyable. Talking to some of the pilots who were eventually to become fighter aces in the Battle of Britain was exciting. My stay at Duxford was however shortlived.

On 20th April 1940 I was posted to No. 4 Bombing and Gunnery School at West Freugh near Stranraer in Scotland. Obviously, urgent demands were being made by squadrons for navigators and air gunners to bring them up to operational standards. After a frightful journey by train in spartan conditions I arrived and saw these huge but antiquated aircraft—Handley Page Heyfords—on which I was to carry out my air gunnery training. Back to the classroom to acquaint ourselves with all the intricacies of the Vickers Gas Operated Gun (V.G.O.), the Lewis Gun and then the Browning .303—incessant stripping and re-assembly—even blindfolded—we were told that we may be faced with such an eventuality if guns jammed in action at night. Certainly nobody 'ducked' this training, we were vitally aware that it could mean life or death to us in the weeks and months ahead. Target practice with camera guns in the classroom followed, with all the complexities of relative speed, bullet trail and drop, and we never envisaged being able to hit a thing.

Came the day to put the theory of gunnery into practice

and we trooped out to the old Heyfords in groups of six. These aircraft looked enormous with their fixed undercarriages and when we climbed aboard we found that we were to conduct our gunnery from either the manually operated dustbin turret slung under the belly or from the scarf ring out in the open in the nose of the aircraft. It was not equipped with inter-com so communication between pilot and gunners was made by a 'runner', who would shout "Fire now," or "Stop firing." He needed strong legs and a loud voice.

The serviceability of these aircraft left a lot to be desired and it was common to climb aboard, the pilot would do his pre-flight tests, declare the aircraft unsafe to fly, and we would off load and troop back to the classroom. Our first airborne exercise was distinctly perplexing, the plane shuddering and shaking across the grass field and staggering into the air at something like 80 m.p.h. A static target on the beach was circled and one by one we took turns at the gunnery stations. Standing at the nose position open to the elements brought tears streaming down your cheeks—goggles were in short supply. The dustbin turret was horrifying, seemingly only supported by a bicycle chain and there was the feeling that jumping down into it would make it part company from the aircraft completely! We looked at the target circle on the beach and the aircraft gave the impression of standing still. It was therefore impossible to miss the target from about 1,000 ft. at the slow speed we were flying and we were all achieving over 90% hits.

On the rare days that the Heyfords and Fairey Battles were serviceable, we underwent further gunnery training in the aspect of relative speed targets, quarter attacks etc. and I had the greatest admiration for the guys towing target drogues to be shot at by we novices. The declared results after each exercise were met with disbelief by the trainees who were either convinced that they had shot the thing to bits or had missed it completely, but it often turned out to be the complete reverse of their expectations. Our last exercise was cut short when the engines failed and we were obliged to 'pancake' ever so softly on the local beach. Having established that our particular course had not fired sufficient rounds to qualify—due mainly to aircraft unserviceability—we were instructed to report to the rifle range to fire off the required rounds with the .303 Lee Enfield rifle at static ground targets. Our experience at West Freugh Bombing & Gunnery School gave us the impression that in any actual combat we would be landing to fire rifles at attacking aircraft! Nevertheless, we were presented with our 'flying bullet' badges to signify that we had qualified as Air Gunners. My log book was certified by a S/Ldr Gray that on 17th May 1940 I had passed as 'Average' with 81.6% Exam. marks and recorded percentage hits in the air exercises of:

Beam Targets—7.5%	Under Tail Targets—3.3%
Relative Speed Targets—14.5%	Quarter Tail Targets—6%
Air to Ground Targets—71%	Total flying time for course—6 hrs 45 mins.

Such was the extent of our gunnery training in those critical times and it did not boost our confidence to meet the Luftwaffe having heard some daunting reports of their prowess at that time.

On 19th May 1940 I was posted to No. 12 Operational Training Unit (O.T.U.) at Benson in Oxfordshire and two weeks later detached to Penrhos in North Wales for further gunnery exercises in Fairey Battles.

This, fortunately, was more realistic training even if it only covered a total flying time of six hours. It gave us the impression of actual battle conditions, especially when the V.G.O. gun jammed on occasions as an 'attacking' aircraft was coming in for a kill and, suppressing the feelings of panic, the stoppage had to be cleared with all possible speed. The weather at that period was excellent, long hot summery days allowing flights every day. It was on one such day that I was released from duty, and ventured to the beach at nearby Pwhelli to cool down with a swim. I recall the beach being virtually deserted and thinking that but for the war it would have been swarming with holidaymakers. I revelled in the warmth and started to swim, after about fifteen minutes turning on my back to find the beach was just a blur in the distance. Unwittingly I had been taken far out to sea by the currents and I realised that it was beyond my capabilities to get back. A mad panic came over me and for a few minutes I struck out like one possessed. Then came a feeling of extreme tiredness, a desire to give up and accept the inevitable. I couldn't bear to look at the coastline so turned on my back and persuaded myself that I would keep going as long as my breath would hold out, hoping like hell that someone would spot me in difficulty. After about twenty minutes of extreme tiredness I seemed to get a new injection of life and the pain barrier dissipated but I did not dare to look again for the beach. Once more I started swimming, and after more than an hour I was able to touch terra firma, with difficulty staggering through the water with the stiffest muscles imaginable, though obviously elated at having 'made it'. Certainly the thought went through my mind that at 19, life was going to be hazardous and perhaps I would be lucky to see my 21st birthday. Needless to say I didn't venture to that beach again!

In the following weeks I received concentrated training in Battles and Ansons, carrying out Cross-Country exercises in wireless telegraphy, ZZ (Blind) landings, D/F (Directional Finding) homing, use of oxygen, formation flying, bombing and gunnery etc.

FIVE

No. 150 Squadron Operations

With a total flying time to date of 62 hours I left O.T.U. (Operational Training Unit) and had four days leave granted before joining my first operational squadron, 150 Sqdn. in 1 Group Bomber Command at the beginning of July 1940. Arriving at Newton in Nottinghamshire some hours late after difficulty in getting a train, I found the aerodrome almost deserted and devoid of aircraft. It was evident that the survivors of the Squadron were still finding their way back from France by whatever means they could, following the fall of France on 18th June. After seven days of waiting and complete inactivity, the surviving crews of 103 and 150 Squadrons from France started to dribble in with their tales of the horrors they had experienced in those last weeks when they were endeavouring to stem the Nazi tide.

They quoted the loss of five aircraft out of six in an attack on the bridges at Maastricht. With new crews arriving from O.T.U. and aircraft (Fairey Battles) flying in daily, the semblance of a squadron was building up again and the crewing-up procedure was under way. It was my good fortune to be teamed up with Harry de Belleroche and Dil Thomas, Pilot and Navigator respectively who were to become fondly known as Rocky and Ginger. After their experiences in France and the withdrawal which in itself had presented such huge problems for them, they could not have been too enamoured with the idea of having a 'rookie' Wireless Op./Air Gunner, but of course they gave me great support and encouragement.

Having been elevated to the lofty rank of Sergeant direct from AC2 (Aircraftman Second Class) on 25th May 1940 I was able to find out from Ginger Thomas during our conversations in the Sergeant's Mess, details of their experiences in a fully operational squadron and the qualities and calibre of other squadron members. Young faces bore the marks of the hardships they had had to endure and they looked far older than their actual years, such were the rigours of their experiences in a comparatively short period of battle conditions after that long period of non-activity known as the 'phoney war' from September 1939.

The decision to promote all non-commissioned aircrew to Sergeant status, purportedly to provide certain privileges during a probable short life expectancy, coupled with the desire to prevent dissemination of information regarding operations and confidential matters to 'other ranks', was not well received by the time-serving NCO's who had spent long years in the ranks as AC2/AC1/LAC/ and Corporal before achieving those three stripes. The influx of large numbers of aircrew—mainly with only one year's service—was strongly resented, and the hallowed Sergeant's Mess was never the same if you believed their arguments. In voting for Mess Committee Members, the dominance of aircrew ensured that they installed their favourites—much to the disgust and chagrin of the 'old sweats'. This attitude became tempered in time as operational casualties followed with the resultant loss of familiar faces and appearances of replacements in the Mess. At this time, resplendent in uniform bearing the insignia of a Wireless Operator's 'sparks' badge, Air Gunner 'flying bullet' and three stripes, and of course enjoying all the hitherto unknown privileges of the Sgts. Mess, one felt suddenly important, the ego was boosted dramatically but there was a pervasive feeling that it was to be short-lived, all too good to be true. Sitting in the comfort of the Mess, listening to the hair-raising experiences of Dil Thomas, Bugs Burrows and Paddy Wildman gave a clue of what was to come. In the confusion of the withdrawal from France, Ginger Thomas and a few other airmen and ground crews had lost contact with the Squadron and were told to trek towards Brest on the West Coast by whatever means they could, in the hope of reaching a ship uplifting survivors for return to the safety of the U.K. Eventually reaching Nantes, they were informed that they should endeavour to embark on the liner *Lancastria*—the 20,000 ton Cunard White Star liner converted to troopship and capable of evacuating 5,000 troops. Imagine their consternation when they found the liner full to the gills and they were refused permission to board. Little did Ginger know his luck for the *Lancastria* was bombed by Junkers 87 dive bombers and sunk within half an hour of the attack with the loss of over 3,000 soldiers, sailors and airmen. June 17th 1940 was a date he would always remember. Further up the coast he was relieved to find a British Destroyer still taking survivors and so was able to be evacuated safely. On 21st June 1940 the Franco-German Armistice was signed and the capitulation to Italy followed three days later.

The air attacks on Britain following the French capitulation were greatly intensified and there was great speculation on the probability of an airborne invasion of Southern England which could only be met by a depleted defence following the debacle in France, and the R.A.F. Fighter Command frontline aircraft were comparatively few in numbers and required time to build up strength. Bomber Command similarly were sadly lacking in numbers of front line aircraft and consequently the effective contribution they could make almost insignificant. We had to pray for time to build up an effective striking force but how much time could we anticipate?

Three weeks after joining 150 Squadron, during which we had flown only nine hours on crew familiarisation, came the day, 25th July 1940, when we were instructed to report to the Operations Room for briefing for our first mission. Our squadron effort was to be only three aircraft to attack an airfield near Antwerp. The total Command effort for the night was to be 166 aircraft to attack seven targets in the Ruhr and various airfields in Holland and Belgium. Our Fairey Battle L5510 was to carry four 250 lbs. G.P. (General Purpose) bombs, two under each wing, so we were told it was vital not to waste the effort, but it did really seem to be an insignificant effort. Briefing over, we returned to the Mess to contemplate our first mission, reflecting on the possibility of our chances of being back in the Mess the following day. With take-off planned for 2350 hours, we experienced at 2100 hours the operational aircrew prior-flight meal of eggs and bacon which was to be a feature of all future operations. One rarely saw eggs as part of the normal diet and it was therefore considered to be a special bonus for risking your head being blown off. What a super incentive!

At 2315 hours we were transported to our aircraft to prepare for take-off and speaking for myself—my pulses were racing and I was sweating more than a little. In pre-flight checks, it was my job to ensure that the radio and intercom were working satisfactorily and that sufficient canisters of ammunition were stored safely. Initially, the warmth within the flying sidcot, fur-lined boots and flying helmet, was rather overpowering but the temperature fell drastically once in the air—especially with the cupola open at the rear of the Battle. The cupola had to be open to enable the VGO gun to be swivelled from port to starboard.

Ginger took up his position as Navigator in the well of the aircraft—a most unenviable position, and sorted out his route maps. Rocky ran up the engine to full power, checked that we were all satisfactory, and then said: "Here we go chaps, good luck!" We bounced across the grass field and at 2355 hours took off for the first of our affrays against enemy-held Europe.

Of the three squadron aircraft assigned to attack Hingene airfield near Antwerp one piloted by Sgt. Pay had to return to base within half an hour with engine trouble. This left ourselves and one aircraft piloted by F/Lt Hugo Beall, a Canadian whose observer was Sgt. Ian Bishop and W/Op.-A/G Bugs Burrows—all ex AASF (Advanced Air Striking Force) veterans at an early age. My brief was to keep a listening watch on the Command frequency at half hourly intervals for possible recalls or diversions, and at my position in the rear of the aircraft—with the cupola open, to man the VGO gun against possible fighter intervention. I recall it being very cold but at the same time sweat was very evident under my flying helmet. Many times I thought that I had sighted interceptors but then realised it was the shadow of our own plane on the cloud. It was a constant switch from 'safe' to 'fire' on the VGO gun but I was determined not to be caught napping. The thoughts that went through my mind varied from 'Have the armourers correctly set the interruptor gear on the gun?'—this enabled the gunner to sweep the area of fire to the rear and quarters without shooting off the tail of the aircraft, to 'How near is my parachute in case I need it in a hurry!' Happily, the flight was uneventful and we dropped our four 250 lb. bombs on target with 7/10ths cloud obscuring results. We returned without incident and landed back at Newton at 0325 hours—our first operation was over. I thought one down and 29 to go—if they were to be as easy as the first—then perhaps I would see my 21st birthday! Ginger emerged with his maps and logs smothered in glycol—this was to be a persistent feature on all future flights, the Battle was notorious for its glycol leaks.

Four nights later on 29th July 1940 we were briefed to attack Waalhaven and took off at 2330 hours with our usual 'magnificent' load of four 250 lb. G.P. bombs. In my anxiety to scour the sky for enemy fighters, I was guilty of missing the group broadcast which had issued cancellation of the operation and instructed all aircraft to return to base. Eventually I informed Rocky of the recall and back we went to good old blighty. With 10/10th cloud conditions it was necessary to obtain homing bearings from Newton and finally we landed and taxied to outside the control tower. Climbing down from Battle L5447, we were met by the C.O., Wing Commander Hesketh who said "Do you realise that you were the only aircraft over enemy territory tonight?" Nevertheless, he was glad to see our safe return and he handed me my first pint of beer which was to be the first of very, very many over ensuing years.

In the next three weeks we were engaged in Army Affiliation Exercises, ZZ landings and bombing and gunnery practice from Catfoss. On 15th August we carried out a North Sea Sweep and whilst there was a risk of interception by enemy intruders this was not counted as an operational mission. A week later our base at Newton was attacked and nine bombs hit the airfield rendering it partly unserviceable but we were able to continue our flights to Catfoss for bombing and gunnery.

One of the bombs dropped by the low-flying Dornier had landed close to living quarters and failed to explode. The airmen were evacuated from the living block and were temporarily accommodated in tents pending the arrival of the bomb-disposal squad. By nightfall the Army disposal squad had not appeared. Two airmen affected by the evacuation had gone to town and returned to base rather the worse for liquor and decided that they would remove the unexploded bomb so that everybody could return to their normal living quarters. They acquired a wheelbarrow and proceeded to manhandle the bomb, apparently it fell out of the barrow several times. The offending weapon was eventually dumped without further mishap. In the sober light of day they reflected on the stupidity of their action but no doubt were amused by the questions constantly asked—"Where is our bomb?" Rumours abounded that they were to be court-martialled but we never did learn of any action against them.

A few days later we experienced more excitement. We had just completed a 'compass swing' to ensure its accuracy when we noticed a 103 Sqdn. Battle, standing outside the main hangar, from which a flame seemed to envelop one wing. There was feverish activity by several airmen who were endeavouring to subdue the fire and to release the four 250 lb. bombs suspended under the wings. An Australian pilot F/Lt. Blom rushed forward to give a hand but the fire spread rapidly and the first bomb exploded with ear-splitting noise, blowing out all the windows in the main hangar and killing the three persons on or near the aircraft, including Blom. As the plane was enveloped in flames, the ammunition exploded in all directions and we threw ourselves to the ground where we stayed until the ammunition expended itself. The unfortunate incident was the subject of most of the conversation in the Mess that night.

With the scare of possible invasion, it was evident that we would use every device to prevent a landing on our shores, even the use of gas. We kitted ourselves out in anti-gas clothing, climbed into the aircraft, then proceeded to spray the surrounding areas—not with gas of course, but with aniseed. On landing, we had to scrub down the fuselage and we rued the day we might have to use gas. Our girl friends in Nottingham were constantly asking us about the sweet sickly smells that were dominant after our aircraft passed over. We were tight-lipped and never revealed the sinister answers.

The army affiliation exercises were most realistic. Large numbers of army formations including mechanised units were 'attacked' at Guilsboro near Northampton, and outside Kettering, then at Royston and Woburn. Attacks were made by diving from 7,000 ft. to 500 ft. simulating German Stuka dive bombing tactics. The pressure in diving thus had the effect of forcing me to the floor of the plane and it was impossible to reach the gun to carry out a strafing exercise. Furthermore, my breakfast came up at ten times the speed of consumption and I rued the day that we would be called upon to dive-bomb the enemy. Many valuable lessons were learned from this exercise.

It was evident to Bomber Command Headquarters that the operational days of Fairey Battles were coming to an end and we all sighed with relief. Whilst we awaited our fate with bated breath, some pilots were notified of their postings to Fighter Command to supplement the squadrons designated to meet the oncoming onslaught in the Battle of Britain.

On 25th August we made our last flight in the Fairey Battle, just as far as Stradishall in Suffolk where we were to join 214 Squadron in 3 Group for a conversion course to Wellington I.C.'s. Rocky had been promoted to F/Lt. and he was to be our Captain, with P/O Paul Carlyon as second pilot, Ginger Thomas as Observer, Sgts. Gutteridge and Bossom as front and rear gunners and myself Wireless Operator/Relief Gunner.

Cross-Country exercises were the order of the day for the next two weeks and having not then flown in a Wellington at night we were surprised to learn that our first 'Wimpy' operation would be on the night of 17th September.

We were briefed to fly in Wellington L7859, take off at 2340 hours to attack invasion barge concentrations at Ostend. After the discomfort of flying in Battles, the 'Wimpy' was luxury indeed, I had a reasonable seat and warmth to operate the TR1154/55 radio receiver/transmitter. The security of having two pilots and armament at front and rear, and armour plate behind my seat gave me much more confidence than I had felt before. Ginger had the luxury of a seat and table to consult his maps and his log was at last glycol-free! We reached the target and sighted the rows of barges but Rocky must have had a lapse of memory as he put the Wimpy into a dive—must have thought he was still in Fairey Battles. The reaction from the crew was immediate! "What the bloody hell!" was yelled from each crew position. It is a wonder that the wings were not torn off—such was the angle of dive! However, we survived and there were fewer barges when we left. The operation was repeated on the nights of 23rd and 24th September against Calais and Le Havre with great success. Paul Carlyon was proving to be a pilot of great ability and quickly gained the confidence of the crew. It was obvious that he would receive captaincy of his own aircraft in the very near future. Paul was a genial giant of a man, and he had actually gone the full distance, 10 Rounds with that great American Heavyweight Boxing Champion Jack Sharkey. With Rocky and Paul, we considered we had the best two pilots in the Squadron.

On 27th September 1940 came the call for 'Ops' briefing at 1630 hours which gave a clue to our next mission being of longer duration—possibly our first against Reich territory itself. Speculation became fact as we trooped into the briefing room in the Ops block to find the large target and route map with the vivid red route tape leading to the Ruhr. The target was to be a railway marshalling yard at Hamm. The Intelligence Officer gave details of the importance of the target and the anticipated areas of flak and searchlight defences. The weatherman gave an optimistic view of conditions en route, over the target and on return to base. The more experienced crews made sly interjections that the weather reports were conjured up from gazing into a crystal ball and later on we were to reach the conclusion that indeed this was near to the truth. Details of bomb load, fuel and armament were outlined and after a few words of encouragement from the Squadron C.O.—the usual "Hit 'em hard lads!"—we broke off for individual briefings on navigation, radio procedures and gunners guidance. The Wireless Leader issued 'colours of the day'—to be fired off in the event of being fired at by our own anti-aircraft defences and/or fighters. The half hourly broadcast by Group headquarters was to be logged and acted on accordingly and radio silence was to be maintained except in dire emergencies. All messages were to be in code for which we were issued SYKO machines for encoding and decoding purposes. Anticipated enemy radio beacons to enable position 'fixes' to be obtained were announced. Every aspect appeared to be covered and transport was arranged to take us to dispersal points at 1915 hours for a take-off at 2010 hours in Wellington IC-L7856. The intervening hour and a half was spent in writing the odd letter, reading, playing cards, emptying pockets of all matter which could be construed as being helpful to the enemy in the event of our being shot down and captured. Boarding the lorry with all our kit to reach our aircraft 40 minutes before take-off, the nervous banter of the crews gave the impression that we were going to a party—a 'party' from which some of us were not destined to return. Standing outside the aircraft, last cigarettes were smoked, one or two lads had a final 'pee' over the tail wheel and then climbed aboard.

Everybody took up their positions, made their usual pre-flight checks and then we heard the first aircraft starting engines. Our turn came and the engines burst into life, were run to ensure no magneto drops and then 'chocks away' and we were taxiing out in a long line of both 150 and 214 Squadrons. In succession, with a green light from the Flying Control caravan the aircraft took off from Stradishall and we were on our way into the unknown.

Once over the sea, the gunners tested their guns, taking care that no other friendly aircraft were endangered by doing so. We reached the enemy coast without event and set course for Hamm. It was not long before we entered belts of searchlights which were blinding in their intensity and one felt that they were only looking for you and you were exposed to the world! At 15,000 ft we experienced heavy flak and saw the black puffs of smoke all round us and could hear the noise of the shell bursts over the sound of our engines in spite of wearing helmets with ear pads. It was, to say the least, unnerving but we pressed on with hope and a prayer. In the run up to the target area it seemed that all hell had broken loose. We seemed unable to lose the searchlight concentration, the sky was filled with bursting shells and lower down we could see the tracer trails of the flak. Ginger in his capacity as Observer encompassing duties of Navigator and Bomb Aimer, had taken up his position in the bomb-well, then proceeded to give his instructions to Rocky—"Left, left, steady, right, steady." If a small correction was required then directions were said quickly and for major corrections the instruction was drawn out. It was an eternity before we heard him say "Bombs away"—with a cacophony of sound breaking out all around us. Paul shouted "Let's get out of here," and Rocky proceeded to throw L7856 around the sky in an endeavour to escape the flak and searchlights. This was eventually achieved and unscathed we set course for home. As we looked back we saw the glow from incendiaries and the flashes of bombs bursting in the target area—giving us immense satisfaction. The gunners traversed their power turrets and kept up an incessant search for fighters. Once across the enemy coast we felt we could relax only slightly but enjoyed the hot coffee from our flasks. All we had to do now was to get back to base and we were looking forward to our special aircrew 'ops' breakfast—eggs and bacon!

Each crew member came on to the intercom to give their assessment of how things had gone, but Ginger told the crew to stop waffling and to keep the intercom clear as night fighters could intercept and any attack could be over in just a few seconds—with possible fatal results unless the gunners could provide for instant sightings and pass instructions to the pilot for evasive action to be taken. Silence became an unwritten rule for future operations.

Challenged by one of our own coastal batteries we fired off the appropriate 'colours of the day' and then reduced height for return to Stradishall. Cloud base was low and Ginger was not too confident of our position, after deviations from given courses, calculations being only by dead reckoning (DR), there being no navigational aids such as radar at this time. DR was affected by windspeed and direction and the science was far from exact. In complete darkness and low cloud, we searched for the tell-tale beacons that would flash the letters identifying our own or other air-bases. We could see none and Ginger requested me to obtain homing radio bearings from base. I tuned into the appropriate frequency and requested QDM (homing bearing) and after a time received the answer—"you are transmitting a split note and cannot determine a true bearing." I retuned my TR1154/1155 and tried again with exactly the same result. Rocky said that fuel was running low and that he needed a course to steer to land at the nearest base. Ginger urged me to help with all possible speed.

In frustration I changed frequency to Cottesmore and requested an urgent QDM. After an interminable period they too replied that I was transmitting a split note and they couldn't determine our position. By now I was sweating profusely and again I tuned and retuned the transmitter without success: then Rocky said that we had come to the end of our fuel, one engine had already failed, and we would have to make a crash-landing. Ginger shouted to me to join him on the floor and to brace myself for the inevitable crash. I did this, placing the log book between my teeth—then there was no further engine noise, just the whistling of air rushing past. Rocky and Paul were fighting to hold the aircraft in a level position. It seemed an eternity but my life flashed through my mind and I prayed that the end would be quick, hopefully not to be enveloped by flames within that geodetic mesh! Looking up from the floor I had a quick vision of trees flashing past and then we struck terra firma. The impact was terrific and Ginger and I were lifted as one, momentarily it seemed that we were suspended in mid-air and then we together crashed through the bulk-head doors, over the main spar and then down to the rear turret. Concussed but still aware of being alive, we tried to struggle to our feet but earth and potatoes had penetrated to a depth of about two feet and progress to an escape hatch was difficult. Our means of escape was through the pilot's hatch over the cockpit. But then panic set in as I saw a red glow from the front of the aircraft and immediately thought 'We are on fire!' Falling down with every step I eventually reached the cockpit to find all other crew members gone, the supposed 'fire' was in fact the red light glow from the light left on over the radio set. I was still convinced that the plane was going to ignite and explode at any second—having seen such things with other crashed Wellingtons. I stood on the pilot's seat to gain exit through the hatch but fell back three times through sheer anxiety. Finally I made it to the roof and couldn't see how far off the ground I was, due to intense darkness. I thought: 'Here goes, two broken legs would be better than a frizzled corpse,' and jumped into the unknown. It was about ten feet to the ground and once I realised I had still two legs, I started to try to break Olympic records in an attempt to get clear of a potential time-bomb. The memory of that morning will remain with me for ever. It did do one thing for me, it gave me confidence just thinking that I had survived such a horrendous experience.

Running away from the site of the crash, which turned out to be at Barton Mills (Suffolk), just a few miles from base, I ran into an Army patrol of three men—one of whom turned out to be a near neighbour of mine when living in Islington—what an amazing coincidence! Shaking almost uncontrollably I was taken to join the other members of crew. Hot sweet tea was distributed and not a lot was said while we drank. Eventually Rocky and Paul both asked me what had gone wrong with the radio, whilst we were being transported back to Stradishall. I said the transmitter appeared to behave normally but for some obscure reason both Stradishall and Cottesmore D/F Stations were unable to determine our position and then fuel and time had run out on us. Back at the Station, I was amazed that the C.O.'s concern was not that we had safely survived the crash but that we had lost an aircraft valued at thousands of pounds. We were then informed that a Court of Enquiry would be held to establish the cause of the crash—obviously with intent to apportion blame to the crew.

A few days later we re-assembled in the hangar to attend the Court of Enquiry and when called in I saw that all the radio equipment from the crash had been assembled and connected for examination.

An officer from the Radio Section then proceeded to tell the Court that he had thoroughly examined the equipment and found it to be in perfect working order. The President then asked the officer to suggest what could have happened to cause a 'split-note' transmission thus preventing a position fix to be obtained. The witness ventured to suggest that Sgt. Wheeler had not correctly tuned the transmitter due to panic at the time. The President was caustic in his remarks to this witness, suggesting that he was not in a position to suggest a 'panic situation' since he had never flown and was therefore not qualified to make such a comment.

Furthermore, he said, Sgt. Wheeler was an experienced Radio Operator and the fact that he had tuned to two different frequencies and got the same result was indicative of something being abnormal—possible atmospheric conditions, low height etc. I was exonerated from blame.

Throughout November and December we underwent training flights with various captains, and at this time further pilots were transferred to Fighter Command to replace pilots lost during the Battle of Britain. Instructors were urgently required and Rocky found himself en route to Rhodesia to pass on the benefit of his considerable experience to trainee pilots out there.

We were then allocated to a crew under the captaincy of F/O Dicky Morton with F/O Freddy Savage as second pilot. At this point Sgt. Fred Denman joined the crew as front gunner replacing Sgt. Gutteridge. Fred—to become known as 'Denny', came from a family of London taxi drivers based in Cricklewood, all being members of the D.O.B. (Done our bit) Club located in that borough.

In December the C.O. W/Cdr. Hesketh departed to be replaced by W/Cdr. C. Paul. I had a great regard for W/Cdr. Hesketh who had greeted me after my very first operational flight in Battles, but W/Cdr. Paul was also to prove a 'gentleman' with a very caring attitude to all under his command.

As part of squadron training, between operations, we would be assigned bombing and gunnery exercises over the North Sea. We would fly to Driffield, then proceed out to sea and carry out such exercises for about an hour. On one such trip, the Captain called me and said: "Drop a flame float or a sea marker for target purposes." The flame float would burn on the surface of the sea and the sea marker would be visible against the normal sea colouring—both providing targets for our air-gunners and bomb-aimers. I went to the flare 'chute and pondered on whether to use the flame float or the sea marker. I selected the latter, pulled out the pin and threw it down the flare 'chute. As I released it, I suddenly realised I had not pushed out the extension which was necessary to take the canister out past the slip stream. The effect was that the canister came back up the 'chute twice as fast, went past my head, hit the roof of the plane and exploded. I was enveloped in clouds of gold dust which then rolled up the fuselage towards the cockpit. The Captain shouted: "What the bloody hell!" Of course we had to abandon the exercise and return to Driffield, where the pilot landed with great difficulty with his obscured screen. As we climbed out on to the tarmac, it was as if we had been sprayed from head to foot with gold paint and I was harangued by the entire crew. Perhaps it was lucky I had selected the sea marker and not the flame float which may have had a more disastrous effect!

On 7th January 1941 we were once again re-united with Paul Carlyon with Freddy Savage as 'second dicky'. We were delighted with this move. Two nights later, in Wellington IC-R1042, we recommenced operations—this time against Rotterdam—a return flight of 3 hours 15 minutes. An uneventful trip during which Paul Carlyon gained the confidence of the crew by his unflappable attitude. His ability was proven a week later when on 15th January we set off to attack naval installations at Wilhelmshaven and found ourselves in cu-nim cloud conditions with huge formations of ice building up on the wings forcing us to descend rapidly. It was not unexpected when we were compelled to abandon the mission and return to base. Of the 96 aircraft operating that night, only one was lost. The heating system in our aircraft failed and the cold was intense and numbing. We were to learn from later missions that the heater system was likely only to work to the extremes i.e. nothing at all, giving freezing conditions, or the other extreme—baking almost to melting point! I don't know which of these extremes I preferred.

Weather conditions precluded our flying operationally again until 10th February when in 'C' for Charlie we made our longest flight yet—to Hanover (6 hrs. 35 mins.). A total of 222 aircraft were committed to this target of which four aircraft were lost and three more were shot down over the U.K. by enemy intruders. It was common when preparing to land that the flarepath would be switched off when enemy fighters were known to be in the area and we had to cruise round with navigation lights extinguished, making it very hazardous with other returning bombers in the same circuit, all with trigger-nervous gunners anxious to strike before being struck down themselves.

The Blohm & Voss U-Boat yards in Hamburg were our next target on 12th/13th March and the force of 88 aircraft included Manchesters and Halifaxes for the first time on a German territorial target. Two nights later it was the turn of Gelsenkirchen to be attacked by 101 aircraft of which 100 returned safely.

In each of these raids on German territory, the anti-aircraft and searchlight defences were superb and caused much consternation among the aircrews—incredulous of their accuracy—and no doubt were responsible for many bombs being scattered.

On 19th March, Sgt. Cliff Cooper went to Buckingham Palace and was presented with the D.F.M. by the King for his excellent record as an Air Gunner in France whilst operating in Fairey Battles. A party to celebrate this well-earned award was held on his return—we needed no other excuse to get sloshed!

Seven squadron aircraft were detailed to attack the submarine base at Lorient on the French west coast and we were fifth away at 1810 hours, routed out over Lyme Regis and arriving over St. Brieuc (France) still in daylight. The 10/10ths cloud en route disappeared over the target area and we bombed from 11,000 ft. The Ground defences and searchlights were ineffective and caused us no trouble and we landed at Newton on the stroke of midnight. One of our aircraft piloted by F/O C. Elliott had not returned to base and whilst waiting into the early hours in the Mess, news came through that the overdue aircraft had evidently got lost in trying to find base and had crashed into a mountain at Blaenau Ffestiniog in North Wales. With the exception of the rear gunner Peter Martlew, all were killed including my good friend Barry Killen. We would miss Barry's fooling around on the piano when he returned after each sortie, and his infectious laughter which had always raised our spirits.

A very good friend of Ginger's and myself was Sgt. Ian Bishop who as an Observer had been with the Squadron since it was reformed prior to the war, was granted a commission and was now to proceed to Canada for a Specialist Navigation Officer's course. But not before we gave him a good send-off in the Mess. Bish had seen action in France and—a nice looking guy—he was respected throughout the squadron and we were sad to see him go—perhaps we didn't see him go as we were all legless after our party. There were to be many more parties thereafter to acknowledge missing friends, promotions and awards for bravery.

With continuing losses of dear friends, it was necessary to dispense with emotions and invariably this was helped through the Mess parties which were arranged for no specific reason. The foolhardy endeavours to walk the length of the Mess with a pint of beer balanced on the head, the battles between opposing sides armed with soda syphons created havoc for the Staff.

On one occasion, we left the Mess for our billets, having consumed more liquor than was good for us but reasonably in control of our faculties—or so we thought! Having donned my pyjamas, I thought that I should relieve myself before retiring for the night. The toilet already being occupied, I decided to venture outside the hut to 'water the flowers'. By this time the booze had obviously taken over and I knew no more until I came to halfway up a huge mound of coke in pouring rain. I was soaked to the skin and my feet were very much worse for wear with cuts and abrasions. It was evident that somehow I had climbed a ten foot high fence to enter the coke compound but I had no idea where this compound was located in relation to my living quarters. I could find no exit and had therefore to resign myself to climbing out over the fence again. This was a painful process but had to be done if I was to avoid embarrassment when daylight arrived. I have no idea how I managed to reach the right side of the wire fence but remember walking in the direction of a glimmer of light chinking through the curtain of a hut. I knocked and entered, to find someone reading in bed. The sight of me must have been a terrific shock to him and he cowered away from me with a nervous, "Who are you—what do you want?"

With difficulty, I explained what had happened and said that I needed some directions to reach my billet. Giving me the general direction in which to head, he was distinctly pleased to see the back of me—I doubt that he ever believed my story!

Many obstacles beset me in the darkness, and my bleeding feet felt as if they did not belong to me. Completely sober by this time, I was cursing my hut-mates for not instituting a search for me. As dawn broke, I reached my hut at last and staggering through the door I made my presence known to all and sundry. Soaking my feet in the bath, two colleagues said that they were aware I had not returned from my 'pee', and had looked around for me but finding no trace, had assumed that I had found a bed elsewhere.

I told them that in the event of another party, they should tie a lump of string around my ankle just in case I should attempt another 'feat' of endurance.

Our 14th operation was on 30th March (1941) when six squadron aircraft were ordered to attack the two German Battle Cruisers, Scharnhorst and Gneisenau—nicknamed 'Salmon & Glukstein'—(famous London store). These were lying in dock at Brest on the French coast. Intense flak and searchlights were encountered in clear conditions but the attack was pressed home. When we returned to base a 'red' warning was on with a suspected enemy intruder in the circuit and once again we were circling the 'drome awaiting clearance. Sgt. Vic Coleman attempted to land and was attacked by cannon and machine gun fire and sustained damage to a landing wheel and petrol tank. He promptly opened up the taps and weaving violently to ward off further attack he diverted to Waddington and landed satisfactorily. We too went to Waddington, not wishing to risk being shot down over our own base. Our Flight Commander, S/L Hugo Beall flew with us on this trip, replacing Freddy Savage who was preparing to receive his own captaincy.

Our next operation on 8th April was a return to Rotterdam to attack oil storage tanks, only five of our squadron aircraft being involved. One of these captained by F/Lt. Frank took a heavy flak battering over the target, lost all of his hydraulics but safely got back to base with bomb doors still open, no undercarriage or flaps but to our delight he made a safe belly landing. Boy, did that crew beat the record in evacuating the wreck! We had, for the first time, Sgt. Sam Huggett as our second pilot. Sam was such a shy reserved person, not reacting to all our usual crew banter, but he was a good pilot.

A return to Brest was our next mission on 13th April and we found 10/10ths cloud over the target and the bombs were released through the cloud with unobserved results. We were getting sick of the sound of Brest and wondered how much longer those two Battleships would survive. I suppose the Royal Navy were content to have them confined to port and not on the open seas to wreak their havoc.

Two nights later, 15th April, five crews were detailed to attack Kiel on the north German coast—an important naval base, and four to the Channel ports. We were airborne at 2040 hours in very good weather conditions, heading out over Skegness to Sylt and Flensburg but on arrival at Kiel 8/10ths cloud covered the target. Intense heavy anti-aircraft fire was set up by the town's batteries. Without radar we were obliged to bomb on dead reckoning and no results were observed so we scorched it back to base landing at 0410 hours.

Three aircraft set out on 17th April for Mannheim but weather conditions were foul and we were unable to locate the target and as we were loathe to bring back our bombs—apart from the hazard of landing with same—we decided to off-load them on an aerodrome near Brussels, encouraged by the sight of a resultant large fire.

It was to be almost two weeks before operating again, undertaking some cross-country exercises with Sam Huggett at the controls during daytime, and evening sorties into Nottingham. The usual haunts for aircrew in Nottingham were 'The Black Boy', 'Flying Horse' and 'The Trip to Jerusalem'. Apart from the booze and the 'line-shooting' about operational experiences, girls of all ages, shapes and sizes were drawn there like magnets and many of the lads failed to reach the last bus back to camp, some trickling in at daybreak. On one such foray I met Hilda Nixey, an attractive blonde who persuaded me on one occasion to take her to the cinema in preference to guzzling beer all evening. As it happened, three of our crew, Denny Denman, Bill Bossom and myself—accompanied by the fairer sex ventured to the cinema but found our vision of the screen obscured by a woman in front with a large hat and a long feather sticking inches upward. We politely asked her if she would remove the said hat. After minutes of endeavour to remove the hatpins, she became irritated and decided finally to leave the hat in situ. This was not good enough to satisfy our party who were by this time in fits of giggles and unable to concentrate on the film. No doubt irritation was also being experienced by the other cinemagoers. It was not long before a pair of nail scissors were produced and with deft fingers the obtrusive feather was snipped. The owner was obviously concentrating on the film and was unaware of the calamity that had befallen her but there was no way that we could contain ourselves so we left not so quietly with glaring looks from the audience and to remarks that "We should grow up and act like men!" With our anticipated life expectancy we didn't wish to 'grow up'.

Walking into the crew room one morning, we spotted that the 'serviceability' board bore the names of girls in Nottingham, many of them familiar to us, with details of their sex prowess, dates when they should be overlooked, whether they were married or not, and whether overnight accommodation was available etc. etc. This information was updated almost on a daily basis and it needed to be consulted before embarking on any blind dates.

Mostly, the crews enjoyed their own company and were content to drink themselves silly and to join in the most bawdy of songs. There was always a piano player available—ready to accept the many drinks bought for him or her in return for hours of musical entertainment. The only difficulty was locating the bar through the thick fog of cigarette smoke. Everybody seemed to smoke in those days—the luxury of dying from cancer never occurred to anybody—it was expected that death could only arrive by violent means.

The last days of the month arrived and after a night flying test in a strange aircraft (R1495) we found ourselves being briefed to attack Kiel again. One of eight aircraft assigned, we took off at 2055 hours, following the coastline down from Kappeln to the target where we found 10/10ths cloud at 10,000 ft. Bombing of any specific target was impossible but the searchlight activity was intense. We decided to let the searchlight crews have the benefit of our considerable bomb load following which there was an immediate extinguishing of all lights.

It was the turn of Cologne on 3rd May but once again cloud came to the rescue of the Reich and the target was totally obscured. Nevertheless this raid counted towards our first tour and we had clocked up our 20th operation—about halfway to the desired total before being 'screened' to take up instructional duty at an O.T.U. (Operational Training Unit).

An uneventful raid on 5th May was to Mannheim and yes, 10/10ths cloud again obscured the target area. Flak was of barrage form and only slight damage was experienced. We landed back at base at 0440 and were content to watch the dawn rise as we hungrily consumed our eggs and bacon.

The 7th May saw us on our way to St. Nazaire, the 'U' Boat base; we were airborne at 0015 hrs, one of ten squadron aircraft detailed. A daylight landing at 0610 hours, debriefing and the usual breakfast. We thought we might become egg-bound if we operated too frequently. The bad news was that R1374, captained by Freddy Savage who had previously flown with us as second pilot, had failed to return. Replacement crews were to arrive in the next 48 hours. No respite for us as that same night we were despatched to Bremen but this time the weather was excellent and the target objectives stood out with complete clarity. All crews were satisfied with their results and we landed unscathed at base at 0455 hours. It was so unusual to bomb in clear conditions, and the crews eagerly scanned the displayed photographs of our bomb plots later in the morning.

Forty-eight hours later (10th May) we were off again, this time to Hamburg, and the weather was perfect. Nine of our aircraft were involved and we crossed the coast at Cromer, then on to Texel on the Dutch coast and then Hamburg clearly seen, ideal bombing conditions. We bombed from 15,000 ft and saw detonations in the target area. It was on this trip that we were concerned to find on entering the aircraft that a number of 25 lb. G.P. bombs were lying loosely on the bed and immediately presumed they had been left there by armourers in error. The skipper Paul Carlyon scotched that idea—saying the bomb racks were full and the 25 pounders were to be released individually through the flare chute by the wireless operator when over the target. I couldn't believe my luck! As we neared the target area, I took up my position near the flare chute, pushed out the extension to allow the bombs to enter the slipstream under the tail section. At the height we were flying it was necessary to plug into the oxygen supply. If one had insufficient oxygen at that height, one was apt to do silly things and act irresponsibly. Having plugged into both oxygen and intercom, I awaited orders to proceed. At this point I found that my oxygen tube was too short to allow me to reach the bombs on the bed without disconnecting from the oxygen supply point over the flare chute. The flak was now becoming intense and accurate, and I could hear distinctly the crump of the bursting shells over the noise of the engines. My priority now was to get rid of those loose bombs as quickly as possible. I disconnected from the oxygen point, moved over to the bed, cradled the first 25 pounder in my arms and moved back to the chute. Plugged back into the oxygen, several deep breaths, loaded the bomb into chute, pulled out the fuse pin and then released it quickly. This operation was to be repeated five times! After the second bomb was released I was becoming tired, the intercom lead was getting caught up in the geodetics, wasn't sure if I was getting enough oxygen in short bursts and generally was in a state of confusion, constantly being urged by the Captain to get rid of those f . . . . . . bombs whilst being coned by searchlights and hammered by flak. The procedure of fetching the bombs, loading them, pulling out the pins and then releasing was too laborious. The last three bombs went straight down the chute with pins still in, and I was glad to see the back of them. I expected that if they landed in one piece, the enemy would treat them with the utmost caution so at least they would have a nuisance value if nothing else. My relief was such that I sat down on the catwalk and inhaled oxygen as deeply as possible. My fuzzy head cleared, and I was then able to tell the skipper that it was a bloody crazy idea to contemplate that performance being a feature of future operations, and bloody dangerous too! I resumed my position at the radio set and listened for the group half-hourly broadcast. The depth of the searchlight defences was incredible and it seemed that we were constantly illuminated in spite of continued evasive action. With the heavy flak around we at least thought we would be safe from fighter attacks. Denny Denman was in the front gun turret and Bill Bossom in the rear turret. I kept a lookout in the astro-dome. We had just emerged from the searchlight activity when Denny said he had to go to the Elsan toilet located in the rear beyond the main spar. I was to relieve him in the front turret. Denny had passed me on his way and I was preparing to go forward to replace him when there was an almighty crack of exploding AA shells and I was convinced we had sustained a direct hit. My reluctance to enter the front turret in those circumstances kept me rooted to the spot. I heard a mumbling over the intercom from Denny and then nothing more. Calling him brought no response so Paul told me to investigate. I clambered over the main spar and nearly fell over Den's body lying prostrate on the floor. In the darkness, it was necessary to feel my way around and I was about to pull his helmet aside to shout in his ear to ask if he was alright and was horrified to find his face a mass of 'gooey' fluid. I thought that he had been hit in the face which seemed a gory mess. I stayed with him until we were clear of flak and on our way home across that awful long stretch of the North Sea of which I had a dreadful fear of having to ditch in. A little more composed and convinced that we had suffered our first casualty, no movement or sound coming from Denny, I knelt down beside him and was aware of this pungent smell which certainly wasn't how I imagined blood to smell. I pulled off his helmet and in the process nearly strangled him with his intercom lead and oxygen tube. I shouted at what I thought was his ear and noticed that he was stirring. He whispered that he had been hit but that he could feel no pain. Yes, sometimes you could be so badly hurt that you were oblivious of pain and in a semi-coma! My hands had become wet with this 'goo' from his face but it smelt like strong disinfectant. My eyes were beginning to focus in the darkness and suddenly I realised what had happened. The proximity of the bursting AA shell had been sufficient to dislodge the Elsan toilet from its mounting. It had hit the roof of the aircraft, struck Denny on the head rendering him unconscious and the Elsan contents had emptied over his face! As he came round I explained my theory—he was unconvinced. We finally landed at base at 5.15 am and on emerging Denny looked as if he had been rehearsing for a minstrel show—he was covered in black disinfectant and smelled atrocious. We were still laughing hysterically during debriefing and when we sat down to our traditional eggs and bacon we asked him to sit at a separate table. It had been an eventful night and one from which Denny was to gain a lot of laughs when repeating his experience over a few jars of beer. Before we got to bed we learned that aircraft 'H' had failed to return with the loss of the crew captained by F/O Spiller. His gunners were Sgts. Vickers and Patterson who were good friends of mine—we had spent some good times together. Three replacement crews arrived the next day—one of which under the captaincy of P/O Landreth was to be posted missing within ten weeks of joining the squadron.

Our 25th operation was achieved on the night of 12th May 1941 when eight squadron aircraft were detailed to bomb Mannheim but weather conditions were so adverse, which made Ginger's dead reckoning navigation vital, that we released our load through 10/10ths cloud on D.R. and no results were observed. The heavy flak barrage was the only thing of note on an uneventful trip but I'm sure Denny welcomed that after his previous experience.

Three days later eight aircraft were ordered to Swanton Morley to operate against Hanover that night. Having been briefed and delivered to our aircraft 'C' for Charlie, we prepared for take-off but on running the engines one was found to have a serious magneto drop. Engine fitters were called but their efforts were to no avail and our trip had to be abandoned. At least, that was one more day to survive. Having reached 25 ops in our first tour, we began to wonder how much longer our luck would hold.

Whilst we stayed overnight at Swanton Morley, back at Newton three aircraft were taking off at 0140 hours for the 'considered' easier target of Boulogne—the channel ports were the usual targets for new captains to 'blood' their crews. One of these captains, newly appointed, was Sgt. Sam Huggett who had flown with us as our second pilot on a number of raids and we had come to treat him as a special friend. A very competent pilot, we had visions of him completing his first tour of ops without mishap. Alas, he completed his attack as scheduled and was returning to base when he lost an engine and finally crashed near Leicester with the loss of five crew members including himself. We all felt shattered at this news. Denny undertook to see Sam's widow, Kay, at the funeral and to pass on our sincere condolences. It was to transpire that Denny, who had become estranged from his own wife, would be seeing a lot more of Kay in future months and years, and they were to eventually marry and settle down in Southend on Sea—until Den contracted cancer of the throat after the war and died in Rochford Hospital.

Another crew on this 'Fresher' trip to Boulogne, newly arrived P/O Topp and crew were to survive this operation but were fated not to return from Hamburg some seven weeks later.

So many crews were not surviving to see ops in double figures. On returning to base from Swanton Morley we were detailed to make a search for a missing aircraft down in the North Sea. The chances of survival after ditching in the sea were minimal but we scanned each dog-leg thoroughly for sight of a dinghy or wreckage. Added dangers of course came from enemy intruder aircraft who would have welcomed the sight of an unescorted Wimpy over the sea. After three hours without result we reluctantly left the area and returned to the comfort of the Mess pitying that poor unfortunate crew if they were still adrift somewhere in that hostile sea.

Two weeks of bad weather gave us a respite from operations and we were occupied with Lorenz Beam exercises at Waddington. Came 2nd June 1941 and we were off again in a force of 25 Wellingtons against Duisburg in the Ruhr. The raid was uneventful and we landed back at base quite unscathed at 0440 hours. After de-briefing and breakfast it was bed in daylight and sleep was difficult with all the usual camp noises; at 11 am I was up again to learn that my promotion to Flight Sergeant was through—another excuse for a celebration drink!

'C' for Charlie was detailed for return raids to Duisburg on successive nights on 16th and 17th June, whilst searchlights and flak were accurate and intensive we were not hit and we survived our 27th sortie. Our C/O W/Cdr. G. J. C. Paul was then posted to Bomber Command H.Q. and W/Cdr. R. A. C. Carter assumed command of the squadron.

A week later we attacked Cologne again without incident and we hit the sack again by 6 am. More serious operations were conducted in Nottingham—our 'targets' being the Flying Horse, Trip to Jerusalem and the Dog & Partridge, from whence we returned without mishap but with rather more 'fuel' than when we set out! The beer must have been heavily diluted in those days as we were easily able to consume eight pints during opening hours of 6 pm to 10.30 pm and we were always first in and last out! It was the turn of Dusseldorf in the Ruhr on the night of 30th June and this being our 29th operation we had reason to believe that we were an experienced crew now and with high hopes of 30 successful 'ops' we could look forward to a 'rest' at an operational training unit (O.T.U.) but I was destined to fly a further nine sorties before this happened.

As we entered July, our second 'dickie', P/O Landreth was given his own crew captaincy and we took on Sgt. Griffiths as his replacement. One sortie against Bremen and two against Cologne were conducted satisfactorily, Cologne having its heaviest raid so far with extensive damage in the centre and east of the city. The success achieved was due to a spell of good weather and clearer conditions. Bomber Command in this era were totally dependant on visual target sightings—there still being no radar navigational aids that were to dictate the course of the air war in later months.

On the morning of 11th July 1941 we got to bed at 6 am after returning from Cologne only to be roused at noon with the news that 150 squadron was moving out of Newton that day—to be re-sited at Snaith, near Goole. We weren't very happy with this news, our stay at Newton being one of comfortable accommodation and messing, with easy access to Nottingham where female company had been very receptive to the glamour 'boys in blue', and where we had built up a good relationship with the licensees.

It was time also to say goodbye to the Flying Banana Morris Car—so called because it was painted bright yellow. This vehicle was devoid of doors, and did sterling service on its excursions into Nottingham. If my memory serves me correctly, Ginger and Ian Bishop were the joint owners, having paid £5 for it. With the lack of private use petrol, I am sure that it ran on a mixture of aviation spirit, paraffin and oil, clouds of smoke issuing on each of its runs. When personnel had lost their last bus back to camp, they would keep an eye open for the Flying Banana and when sighted in the early hours of the morning would leap onto the running board and hang on for dear life. The number of bodies in and on the vehicle sometimes was beyond belief. On one occasion, approaching the West Bridgford area, with bodies hanging on in all directions, the Flying Banana failed to negotiate a roundabout and went straight on up and over this grass mound. Bodies were falling off left and right but the vehicle was not allowed to stop—it might not have started again. It would continue its non-stop journey back to camp—stopping finally in a cloud of smoke at the

Guard Room for identity checks and then having to be pushed to its resting place until the next excursion. I can't recall any bother with the Service Police and I think the C.O. took a low profile. He was surely aware of the notoriety of the Flying Banana but perhaps thought it was an outlet for his crews from the tensions of operational flying. I can still hear the loud cheers from bystanders in the streets of Nottingham as it passed on its way.

The Banana didn't bear a tax disc, Ginger always retaining postal orders to the value thereof for the possible eventuality of being challenged at which stage he would say: "It's in the post, Officer." This happened at Ratcliffe, Notts. when confronted by the law and the pet answer was offered but one of the twelve occupants of the car shouted, "Get some Berlin time in, Copper!" The irony was that none of us had yet been to Berlin, but the remark obviously riled the Constable and consequently cost Ginger and Bish a week's wages. Ginger recalled that he took it to a race meeting one day and that it went faster than the horses he backed that day. One wonders whether the sporting girls of that era are still alive and remember the 'trophies' they left behind in that faithful old motor!

We arrived at Snaith at 3 pm and were horrified to find a newly constructed airfield with Nissen hut accommodation and clouds of dust blowing everywhere. The whole place was in violent contrast to the peace-time set up at Newton and we were all shattered with the conditions, and at the thought of having Goole, the nearest town, as our social activity base. We hardly had time to settle in than we were briefed to attack Bremen, taking off at 2235 hours into thick cloud. Reaching operational height we found ourselves icing up, it was forming up in layers on the wings and it was most uncomfortable. We finally reached the target area and released our bombs with intense relief on Vegesack near Bremen. Seven hours and ten minutes after take-off we landed at Mildenhall to where we had been diverted because of fog at Snaith. After all the uneventful flights from Newton, we visualised that probably our luck would change after having moved to a new base.

The next operation on 21st July 1941 was to be our most hair-raising experience. Entering the briefing room, we looked expectantly at the operations map and saw the red route ribbon targetting to Frankfurt—our first raid on that city. We were airborne at 2210 hours and wondered if we were destined to return to Snaith in the early hours of next morning. The usual searchlight and flak activity was experienced near and over the target but once having released our considerable bomb load we felt relief and thought it was just a matter of getting home now—hopefully without incident. Not long after leaving the target, it was apparent that our starboard engine was not functioning satisfactorily. Paul was concerned that the engine was sounding like a bag of old bones, and said that the oil was obviously not getting through to it. We gradually lost height and Paul directed Denny and myself to operate the manual oil pump located behind the main spar, in an effort to get oil through to the engine. We found, in turns, that the manual pump was almost inoperable, it took immense effort to force it one way and then the other. It was intensely cold and our fingers became numb and we experienced cramp in our legs whilst in the crouching position. It was obvious that our efforts were not working, we could hear tremendous grinding noises coming from the engine and the strain was causing the plane to fly crab-like. Sparks and fire were spitting out from the engine cowling and we were losing more height. I had visions of having to ditch in the North Sea and cursed the possibility of our coming to the end of our luck on our 34th operation.

The noises were becoming more pronounced and Paul was having great difficulty in maintaining course and height. Something drastic was obviously going to happen and it did—with flames and sparks and tremendous grinding within the engine, the propellor with an accompanying section of engine suddenly tore itself free and spun forward and upwards, fortunately, to disappear over the tail and downwards to the North Sea. If, in its final torment it had spun into the fuselage then without doubt I wouldn't have been around to pen this report! As it happened, the aircraft flew much better without it although we were still losing height and we were concerned at the risk of not reaching the mainland. I was instructed to send out 'Mayday' SOS signals—breaking the usual radio silence because of our dire circumstances. We aimed for the nearest coastal point and it seemed an eternity before we made landfall and made a successful one-engine landing on the grass field at Marham in Norfolk. We ran to a halt, clambered out to gaze at the gaping great hole in the engine nacelle and the surrounding ground crew stood there mouthing their amazement. It was not until very much later that Ginger informed us that we had a 1,000 lb. bomb hang-up still in the bomb-bay and that we had unknowingly made a fairly heavy one-engine landing on the bumpy grass 'drome which might easily have dislodged the bomb. Ginger's character was such that he would have carried a guilt-complex over this incident but the crew immediately dismissed this notion out of hand by reason of his wonderful dedication to the job in hand, and hadn't he always navigated us to and from the target so expertly, and got us back to friendly territory time and time again in spite of the many hazards and diversions? So, we thought: "Well, we have got charmed lives, haven't we?" Furthermore, we had taken off from Snaith on two operations and not yet been able to land back there! Was this to be a feature of future operations from there?

Two days later, 24th July 1941, we realised why we had for three days undertaken local formation flying. We just couldn't believe our ears when the C.O. said that six crews were to participate in a daylight operation against the German battleships Scharnhorst and Gneisenau lying at anchor in the French port of Brest. A total of 150 aircraft were planned to make the attack in formation but at the last moment this had to be changed because of the departure of the Scharnhorst to La Pallice. The force to Brest was then to be composed of 100 aircraft of which three were to be Flying

Fortresses flying at 30,000 ft in the hope of attracting German fighters prematurely. Then 18 Hampdens escorted by three squadrons of Spitfires with long range fuel tanks were to attack in anticipation of drawing off more enemy fighters. Finally, the main force of 79 unescorted Wellingtons from Nos. 1 and 3 Groups were to attack in the final wave.

This was to be our first daylight operation and without fighter escort and in the knowledge that our formation flying technique was far from efficient, and enemy fighter prowess was widely known, we did not give much for our chances. As a diversion for this raid 36 Blenheims all escorted by Spitfires were to attack Cherbourg Docks in the hope of drawing German fighters from the main raid. Very apprehensive, we took off at 1050 hours and it took quite some time before our six aircraft could take up some semblance of a formation and set course. The weather was good and visibility excellent, there being no cloud in which to hide in the event of attack.

The German fighter opposition was stronger and more prolonged than anticipated by Group H.Q. but the crews involved had not shared their view. We were struggling to maintain formation and then found that our oxygen supply failed. With the target area sighted ahead with the bursting flak—our engine-driven generator failed and discussion followed on the situation pertaining. With the generator out of action, so many of our electrics would not function and more importantly our bombs would not release. Having come so far, naturally we were disappointed but had to abandon our mission and turn for base. The remainder of the force pushed home their attack but were badly mauled by the German fighter attacks. Ten Wellingtons were shot down—12½% of the total force but six hits were claimed on the Gneisenau. Of the 15 Halifaxes attacking La Pallice, five were shot down and all the remainder damaged but five direct hits were registered on the Scharnhorst putting her out of action for four months. Two of the 18 Hampdens were lost to fighter attacks. It was considered a highly successful operation but with heavy losses. We landed back at base at 4 pm somewhat disappointed but comforted in the knowledge that we had survived our 35th mission. Each operation now was tempting fate—how much longer could we survive when so many crews were coming to grief before reaching double figures of ops completed? The strain was telling on each crew member now and each flight seemed so much harder than ever before.

This was to prove Ginger's last operation of his first tour. He was to go on seven days' leave before going to Canada for his prestigious Specialist Navigation Course. Sadly we were to lose a super Navigator and friend. I think we wished that the rest of us could say 'finis' to our first tour of operations, but this was not to be.

Paul was promoted to F/Lt. and we celebrated this fine Captain's new rank and thanked our lucky stars that we had been fortunate to be crewed with such a competent pilot and skipper.

Still anticipating news from Group H.Q. that our first tour of ops was over we found ourselves briefed again for yet another raid on Cologne. Thunderstorms and severe icing were experienced again and we could not locate the target through 10/10th cloud. We turned for home with our bomb load still intact and then a partial cloud clearance enabled us to see the outline of Courtrai airfield and down went our full load. They must have wondered why they were singled out by a lone aircraft.

Still no news from Group H.Q. and we were airborne again, this time to Frankfurt which had bad memories for us with our previous raid on this target. Very good bombing results were obtained by the 65 Wellingtons and 33 Hampdens inolved and only three aircraft were lost. One of the crashing bombers went straight into a rubber factory employing over 2,000 people.

On 8th August 1941 we were assembled in the C.O.'s office to be told at long last that our operation that night was to be our last and that we were then to be 'rested' at an

O.T.U. The target was Hamburg, not the easiest of targets for our last excursion and we all wished each other good luck and promised ourselves a party if we were fortunate enough to return. We had come to rely on each other so much over a period of one year and had become the staunchest of friends, we almost regretted the necessary split-up to various stations after this last flight together. We reached the enemy coast and experienced flak for the last time and as one engine was not functioning we were forced to abandon our task at Groningen. However disappointing this last sortie was, we had survived where so many crews had not and when we taxied to our dispersal we climbed out of 'C' for Charlie, all kissed the ground in thankfulness, embraced our faithful ground crew and invited them to a final party to show our appreciation of their marvellous service and dedication. The rivalry between the respected ground crews was great and they would all uphold the merits and achievements of their aircrews. While we were fully engaged on flying operations, the ground crews invariably had to hang around, sometimes in the coldest of weathers awaiting our return. Their smiles on our return were indicative of their delight that we had brought *their* aircraft home safely although sometimes with varying degrees of damage.

We were saddened to learn that P/O Landreth and crew were lost in the Frankfurt raid which meant that we had lost all the earlier second pilots on our crew when they had received their captancies.

Some three weeks elapsed at Snaith before our postings came through but we had finished our flying commitment with 150 squadron. Finally, on 28th August 1941 we left Snaith and I found that Denny and I were to be instructors at No. 27 O.T.U. based at Lichfield in the Midlands. It was a delight that I had one good friend from the crew to share our new experiences as instructors. We all expressed the hope that the war would be over before we had to undertake a second tour of ops, but that seemed highly unlikely as the war had gone badly for Britain—virtually on her own but for the gallant help of the Commonwealth. However, against all odds we had survived Dunkirk, the Battle of Britain, and in a smallish way were hitting back at the Reich with limited Bomber forces which compelled the enemy to retain Forces in defence which could have been so usefully employed in other theatres of war.

I was now 21 years old, had completed 38 operations, was still fit and unscathed, and furthermore was in love with Mollie who had been a work colleague when we were employed at Herbert & Sons Ltd., at Edmonton in North London.

Rocky (Harry de Belleroche) had gone to Upavon prior to posting to Rhodesia for instructional duties. Ginger had gone to Canada and Paul was posted to 214 Squadron and had to say goodbye to his faithful bulldog Pickwick. This animal didn't show a lot of affection but was always awaiting Paul's return from flying, sitting outside the Control Tower until satisfied his 'guvnor' was safe and then waddling back to the Mess to await his breakfast.

SIX

O.T.U. Screening

Operational flying having been completed, Denny and I travelled to R.A.F. Lichfield to become Screens (Instructors) for what we thought would be a 'rest' period but was to be in fact far from restful, having to fly with pupil crews which we considered at times to be far more dangerous than flying over enemy territory. It was now August 1941 and for the next 20 months we were to be part of No. 27 O.T.U., training the ever increasing numbers of aircrew including young men from all parts of the Commonwealth—from Canada, Australia, New Zealand, South africa *et al*. My total flying hours up to completion of my first tour of 38 operations amounted to 416 hours of which half had been night flying.

We were welcomed by W/Cdr. H. F. du Boulay the Officer Commanding 27 O.T.U. Training Wing who made it clear that our joy-riding days were over and that we would be expected to return to the standard of discipline that he considered had lapsed on operational stations. Failure to attend lectures and training sessions punctually or being late for flying programmes would bring appropriate extra duties. Denny and I realised that life away from an operational squadron was likely to be hard to take after the many privileges we had enjoyed over the last year.

Having made our spartan billet more accommodating with pictures of the reigning pin-ups—Betty Grable, Rita Hayworth and Larraine Day, our thoughts turned to transport so that we could observe the local talent and of course, anybody with a means of transport could have a distinct pull with the birds, who always seemed to live in all the outlandish places. With the constant comings and goings of personnel, the odd car or two became available and sure enough for the princely sum of £25 we secured another Morris 12 (which reminds me I never did get the £12.50 being Den's share!) I recalled nostalgic memories of the 'Flying Banana'.

After training sessions on the manner in which our experience could be imparted to the 'rookie' crews, it was evident that we would not be flying regularly with experienced pilots. An experienced navigator or wireless operator could be part of a pupil crew and this was somewhat perplexing when we saw some of their take-offs and landings, to say nothing of their navigational abilities on some of the long cross-countries, sometimes over the North Sea where there were the ever present dangers of interception by enemy intruders.

London had been subjected to heavy air raids, the Russians were in full retreat to the gates of Moscow and things looked bleak with no prospect of an end to war for years ahead. All we could hope for was a miracle, but one redeeming fact was that a spirit of comradeship was established between all classes and there was a willingness to help anybody with anything—something we had never experienced prior to the war.

Came December 1941, and we were flying long cross-countries of up to six hours duration, sometimes by day and some by night, with the usual bombing, gunnery and wireless exercises carried out to further the training of the pupil crews who were anxious to join an operational squadron at the earliest opportunity. They never reckoned the odds of surviving beyond 12 operational sorties. Having survived ourselves, we were anxious that they should receive the best training we could provide from our own experience. However, it was a daunting task, thoughts of all these young lads facing up to the many strengths of the Luftwaffe and the tremendous defences that the Germans had established in the occupied territories—unknown as yet to these keen but green crews.

We were looking forward to our Christmas celebrations but dismayed to find on the flying programme notice board that we were due to fly on the night of Christmas Eve. We took off at 2205 hours on a cross-country flight of four hours, wishing each other a "Merry Christmas" as it turned midnight. Retiring to bed finally at 3.30 am we were awakened at 9 am with the news that the N.C.O.'s on camp were to 'wait' on the other ranks at their Christmas Dinner. Nevertheless, it was most enjoyable and we had a lot of fun—at least it was a way of saying thank you to all the lads—some of whom spent long cold hours out on dispersal points awaiting our return from night flying. The day after Boxing Day we were back in full swing again with another five hour cross-country.

On 16th January 1942 I was granted seven days' leave, met Mollie at Kings Cross Station and went to see her parents at Walthamstow. Sleeping arrangements meant that I had to sleep in the Anderson air-raid shelter in the garden, and it was a pleasure when daylight came and one could emerge from the shelter with its condensation streaming down the corrugations. The weekend covered visits to my father, my brother and his wife, and to Nan and George at Kings Cross. They were all anxious to hear of my experiences and listened avidly to the news from the warfront. By this time my Mother had left my Father. Mollie and I felt that we were deeply in love and in spite of the apparent hopelessness of the war situation, the very slight possibility of ever having a home of our own, we thought that we wanted to be together at every opportunity. There was the strong possibility of my succumbing to the dangers of flying each day or night, the probability of Mollie being killed or maimed in the constant air-raids on London—without our having enjoyed the pleasures of consummating our love for each other. With the odds against us, I proposed to her and she accepted without hesitation. Her parents Kit and Bert thought we were 'bloody fools' but raised no objections except to say, "You've both got nothing and probably won't ever have anything in the foreseeable future!" Like excited kids, we had to tell everybody we were tying the knot, and went to our good friends Stan and Elsie Kitchen at Edmonton and they opened a bottle to celebrate the good news. Stan had been my boss at Herbert's before the war. The next morning we went to Leyton Registry Office to obtain the marriage licence at a fee of seven shillings and sixpence (37½p) and then hurried to the jewellers—Wingers in Walthamstow—to buy the wedding ring. Mollie chose a white gold ring and we were both very happy indeed. Next day, Thursday 22nd January 1942 we were married by the Registrar, Mollie's parents attending with my brother Fred and his wife Josie, and Stan and Elsie Kitchen. It was a quiet affair, there not being the means for a feast and our wedding presents comprised of three bread boards—there was nothing else of any substance available. We went to Fred's flat at Enfield in the evening and spent our wedding night there. The thought of returning to camp the next day was depressing and I could only think of my next leave—whenever that would be. In pouring rain I caught the train at 11.55 pm on Friday and a few tears were shed.

Arriving back at Lichfield at 8.30 am, I went straight to the Accounts Section and registered my claim for marriage allowance. Needless to say, I went to bed early that night, knowing I was down to fly the next night. Taking off on Sunday at 2245 hours to fly up and down the Irish Sea, it was bitterly cold, the aircraft heating having failed, and I longed to be back in my billet so that I could write to Mollie—it would not matter that it would be in the early hours of the morning and Denny would say that I was crazy! Letters passed between us almost on a daily basis, goodness knows what we had to say.

On 5th February, Mollie's birthday, we were informed that some of us were being transferred to the satellite aerodrome at Tatenhill and we spent two days ferrying aircraft and equipment. It was a typical satellite 'drome with Nissen hut accommodation and with sparse facilities. Den and I moved in and made ourselves as comfortable as circumstances would allow. Den's cigarette consumption went up to 30 a day. I swore never to smoke whilst I was on flying duties—I always had this feeling that sometime somewhere I would need all the breath I could muster—particularly if I was forced down into the sea. The majority of aircrews seemed to smoke and I was constantly being pressed to partake of their Park Drive or Woodbines—I never did succumb during six years of war. Pay day was every Thursday and I received the princely sum of £2 which invariably disappeared by the following Monday after boozing excursions with Den and Ricky (Sgt. Rickard) to the New Inn. The old Morris 12 we called 'Gertie' was doing sterling service ferrying us to Burton on Trent where the pungent smells from the breweries hung over the town.

Den and I planned a journey to London in Gertie which meant acquiring adequate fuel—the usual mixture of aviation spirit, paraffin and oils. We planned to leave at 8 pm but then found ourselves detailed for night flying. It was agreed that regardless of what time we landed we would proceed directly without having our night flying meal. It was the most bitterly cold night and having no anti-freeze in the radiator Den decided to cover the engine with his greatcoat as a measure of protection. We took off hoping that there would be some excuse for aborting the exercise and returning early. No such luck, we even strayed off course and found ourselves in the middle of a balloon barrage over Birmingham. Searchlights probed the sky for us and when the anti-aircraft guns opened up it was as if we were back on operations. We were relying on the cable-cutters fitted on the leading edges of the wings to cut the cables if we were unfortunate enough to become entangled. Fortunately the flak was not as accurate as we had become used to over the Reich. A very anxious ten minutes was spent with many and varied suggestions being voiced over the intercom.

Eventually we were clear and proceeded to complete our exercise. We landed back at base at 3 am, handed our flying kit to a dumbfounded pupil crew, said we were now on our way to London and went over to Gertie, who was by now completely iced up. It took an eternity to defrost her but she finally burst into life and Denny and I were on our way. We had been driving about 20 minutes, talking about the events of the night when smoke started pouring out of the bonnet and we skidded to a halt on the icy road. We lifted the bonnet and flames burst out into the cold morning air. It was only then that we remembered Den's greatcoat covering the engine and when the flaming mass was removed and thrown on to the roadside we both burst into fits of laughter. By this time the coat was reduced to two sleeves and a collar. No serious harm appeared to have been done to the car so Den wrapped a long woollen scarf around his neck and we were off again. We wondered if any further calamity could befall us that night. Sure enough at Stoney Stratford the engine was coughing and spluttering just as we were approaching a garage which was closed and all in darkness. Grinding to a halt, it was obvious that we had run out of fuel—regardless of the fuel gauge reading a quarter full. We considered the possibility of acquiring fuel by any means, having no coupons for the drastically rationed commodity. Having lost the toss of a coin, I assumed the unenviable task of knocking up the garage proprietor. A woman leaned out of an upstairs window and asked if we realised the time and what on earth did we want. With my fingers and legs crossed, I said that I had just come down from flying, had a message to say my mother was seriously ill in London and didn't realise our petrol gauge was faulty, but needed to get to London urgently. She was clothed only in a nightdress and dressing gown, and proceeded to pump three gallons into the tank, then asked for the coupons. We searched through pocket after pocket without success of course, and she was complaining bitterly of the cold, finally suggesting that we drop them in on the return journey, she beat a hasty retreat back to her warm bed. We thanked her profusely and started off again for our destination at Cricklewood in North West London. Gertie gave a last gasp at Watford and we despaired of reaching Cricklewood—was it all worth it?—Den made a telephone call to his father—Pops Denman who had a taxi-cab business in London, and without ado Pops was on his way to us for a rescue mission. We finally reached Gladstone Park Gardens where Mrs. Denman—Den's mother, prepared a wonderful breakfast for us. She was a lovely person who did everything to make us comfortable. Full of laughter, with her Devon accent, she was telling all her neighbours that her 'boys' were home from the war and nothing was too good for them.

Den's father and grandfather were long-established London taxi cab drivers so it was fitting that we should join them at the D.O.B. Club in Cricklewood where all the cab drivers congregated. Many interesting stories of their experiences were exchanged, and for us lads in aircrew—free drinks came from all quarters, we just couldn't spend a single penny and their generosity was overwhelming. The London cab driver had a character all of his own, and it was an experience to hear of their many exploits during the blitz. They exemplified the true London Cockneys with their extreme courage, good witty humour and their great generosity in times of adversity. I always enjoyed my visits to Cricklewood where I was made to feel that I was part of a big happy family. Since the outbreak of war, Denny had become estranged from his wife, probably irreconcilably following the tragic death of his daughter as a result of scald burns. I only ever saw his wife Jessie on one occasion and couldn't help feeling very sorry for her. She was an attractive woman for whom the war had done no favours, the loss of a husband and daughter must have been traumatic. Such was the lot of so many families in those dark days. A school-time boyfriend of Mollie's—a Jack Avant—had completed his aircrew training in Canada but was killed shortly after his return to the U.K. This was a sad blow to Mollie and her parents who had such a high regard for the lad. Mollie still retains his last letter to her.

Life on O.T.U. was just bearable after all the excitement of being part of an operational squadron, the constant circuits and landings, and the monotonous cross-country flights by day and by night almost driving one to distraction. There were the odd compensating factors of course and on the occasion of non-flying due to inclement weather, the powers-that-be were hard put to know how to occupy our time. Somebody one morning had a bright idea. We were sitting in the flight crew room, huddling round the hot stove which always emitted tear-inducing smoke, and we were discussing topics of interest—mostly girls—when the door burst open and the Orderly Officer announced that we were 'going for a ride'. We were instructed to empty our pockets of any money which would be returned to us later. Pupils and Instructors alike, we were then loaded into closed-in trucks and were driven around the countryside for about an hour, having no clues as to our final destination. Finally drawing to a halt, we were unloaded and then informed that we had to find our way back to camp on foot—without even knowing where we were starting from. Without money to purchase bus or train tickets, and in the knowledge that locals would be reluctant to provide route information due to the scare of enemy infiltrators who were likely to dress in allied uniforms, this task seemed formidable. This foray was not likely to be repeated however, some personnel resorting to stealing cycles or other means of transport, some finding a local inn where they were content to drink on the basis of signing a promissory note and not being in a hurry to relocate the camp. The sum total was that those who did find their way back were followed by the local constabulary registering complaints that various methods of transport had been abused. Some of them didn't even reach camp until well into the next day and the charge sheet was longer than it had ever been before. The exercise was deemed a failure and was not likely to be repeated. Back to 'fire watching' around the crew room stove. The crews from 'A'

Flight decided one morning to cause some excitement in the 'B' Flight crew room. Whilst the 'A' Flight bodies were clustered around the stove to keep warm, reading their lurid magazines and morning mail, completely oblivious of anything going on outside except perhaps awaiting the call to the mobile N.A.A.F.I. wagon, 'B' Flight were wending their way along the roof of the pre-fab huts to the smoke stacks in the 'A' Flight hut. From within, it sounded as if the sparrows and pigeons were wearing studded boots along the roof. The next sound was the tinkle-tinkle of some objects dropping down the smoke stacks, then momentary silence. It transpired that the 'objects' were Very cartridges which, having entered the glowing embers within the stove then ignited and with a big bang and a whoosh flew out in all directions from the open flap of the stove. Colours of the day with accompanying clouds of smoke filled the crew room and there was a mad stampede for the door. Coughing and spluttering, the bodies poured from the hut to be greeted by jeers and cheers from the roof where 'B' Flight were still lodged. They were then bombarded by mud or anything that came to hand, so a good time was had by all. The danger aspect was not considered, it was interpreted as just another interlude to offset the boredom that prevailed on non-flying days. The incident obviously came to the ears of the C.F.I. (Chief Flying Instructor) with the result that the lecture programme was stepped up. All manner of pranks were engaged in for some diversion. On occasions, entering the toilets one would find the toilet rolls would be festooned over the pipes near the ceiling and then some 'clot' would strike a match and set light to them. The riot act would then be read once again, to be forgotten two or three days later.

The usual routines were continued into May 1942 and on the 29th it was apparent that something out of the ordinary was about to happen. The ground crews were being pressed like mad to ensure the full serviceability of all the aircraft and air testing was more prevalent. Parachutes had to be taken for closer examination and leave passes were cancelled, so something 'big' was happening. At 10 am the next morning we were formed into crews, mostly comprised of instructors with a sprinkling of the more advanced pupils and then allocated aircraft. I was assigned to Wellington IC-No. 1645 under the captaincy of F/O Temperley with whom I had flown on some training exercises. Shortly after, we were in the air for an hour's formation flying and air testing. Our formation had to be seen to be believed, and with rumours of a daylight raid to be carried out in these clapped out Wellingtons which had seen better days, we weren't too happy. At 1830 hours we were summoned to the briefing room in the Operations Block. The wall chart area was covered by a cloth and the crews sat there fidgeting awaiting the C.O.'s arrival to announce what was in store for us. Finally, from the back of the room came the order "Attention" and all personnel leapt to their feet as W/Cdr. Jarman entered with S/Ldrs. Bamford and Burberry. We were greeted with the news that the C. in C. Bomber Command—'Butch' Harris was mounting the first raid in which over 1,000 bombers were to be unleashed on the Reich. This could only be achieved by supplementing the operational squadrons with aircraft from O.T.U.'s Coastal and Training Commands.

The concealing cloth was removed and revealed that our target was Cologne. It was announced that only 90 minutes would be allowed for 1,000 plus aircraft to pass through the target area. The dramatic figure of 1,000 planes was something like two and a half times the usual complement of aircraft available for night operations. The main danger was the prospect of collisions but this was an acceptable risk to get the bomber stream through the night-fighter boxes as quickly as possible, to swamp the anti-aircraft defences and to put down such a concentration of H.E. (High Explosive) and incendiaries in a short period that fire services would be overwhelmed and large areas would be consumed by the fires. The O.T.U. Groups were providing 365 aircraft including Wellingtons, Hampdens and Whitleys. It was suggested that the loss factor of 10% or about 100 aircraft would be acceptable for this size operation. With the late withdrawal of the Coastal Command contribution it was necessary to make up numbers with totally trainee crews. The final total dispatched was 1,047 aircraft.

The days of specific targets had gone, and with such a concentration of bombers in so short a space of time there would be no question of evasive action from flak or fighters due to the greatly higher risk of collision with devastating effect on probably many friendly aircraft. Sitting in the Mess prior to take-off, the topic of conversation was dominantly on the question of the adequacy of our aircraft, used day in and day out on training by various crews.

We took off at 2230 hours and it seemed as if the sky was full of black shapes, gun testing had been disallowed because of the density of the formations. We staggered up to 11,000 ft in our weary I.C. but with the bomb and fuel load it just wouldn't go any higher. This would make us a target for the accurate light flak. We were not alone, some old Whitleys were below us and a lot slower and this was a slight encouragement for us. Crossing the enemy coast, we were soon illuminated by searchlight batteries and we felt totally exposed. Aircraft were above and below and on all sides, impossible to take weaving action. Approaching the target area, all hell broke loose and there was no question of overshooting and going round for a second run. In running up, I was located in the astro-dome and I could never recall having been so scared. Many aircraft above us with their bomb doors open revealed stocks of bombs which when released were more than likely to land on the aircraft below. At the point of release, there were showers and showers of incendiaries and H.E.'s passing us on all sides. These obviously accounted for the many explosions around us with many planes ploughing and plunging in big balls of flame into the target area. It seemed like one sea of flame on the ground and I felt sick for the poor devils below and the terrors they must have been experiencing. We sighed with relief after our bomb load had gone down and wondered whether Cologne's wonderful cathedral had been obliterated. The return flight was mainly uneventful and we eventually landed at base at 4.30 am. De-briefing and breakfast occupied the next two hours and thankfully we climbed into our beds at 7 am. It was announced that the raid had been a success, Cologne Cathedral had survived, amazingly, and losses totalled 41 aircraft—3.9% of the total force operating. We thought how glad we were to get this 'one-off' operation over and could get back to our usual mundane but safer task of training. It was not to be, for two nights later the effort was to be repeated, this time against Essen in the Ruhr and we were to suffer all the same agonies again. This flight duration was five and a quarter hours, but due to the considerable haze over the target it was not as successful as the Cologne raid and bombs were well scattered. Thirty one of our aircraft were lost out of a total of 956 dispatched—3.2%—which was lower than expected.

It seemed to us that if we were to operate we may just as well be back on a fully operational squadron with the best available aircraft and not lumbered with clapped-out training types with a lesser survival potential. As it transpired, we were soon back to our normal instructional routine and the thought of further 'ops' had disappeared. That is, until 30th July when we were detailed once again, this time to Dusseldorf and I was assigned to F/Sgt. Chidgey, an exceptionally good pilot who originated from the West Country. We took off just before midnight and landed back just after 5 am. Our O.T.U. contribution to the raid totalled 105 aircraft and our losses were heavy—over 10.5%. We now resigned ourselves to being called for 'ops' at any time in the future, there was no guarantee that being on a Training Station would relieve us of this likelihood.

SEVEN

The Yanks are Coming

America's entry into the war followed the Japanese attack on Pearl Harbour on 8th December 1941. We wondered how soon the U.S.A. would be involved in the European sector and how quickly we in Bomber Command could expect their support.

It was in August 1942 that the first B17E Flying Fortresses of the U.S. Eighth Airforce appeared, and there was much speculation as to what success they were likely to achieve and how much they would relieve RAF Bomber Command in the weeks and months to come.

On 19th August we were summoned to the C.F.I.'s office and volunteers were invited to be detached to the American units based at Bovingdon near Hemel Hempstead in Hertfordshire. This was for instructional duties on RAF procedures and was to last for about a month. I put my name forward for signals attachment together with 'Bugs' Burrows and Johnny Cartwright, Denny volunteered for aerial gunnery duties and a number of pilots and navigators completed the detachment detail.

We arrived at the base on the next day and were allocated our quarters. The Americans made us most welcome and invited us to use their Aircrew Mess and PX facilities. The quality of food was exceptional when compared with our previous diet. Bowls of fruit, hitherto unseen, were free-standing throughout the Mess Hall and naturally we weren't slow to tuck in. The visit to the PX was an eye-opener, cigarettes in cartons of 200 and chocolate and candy-bars that could be purchased for next to nothing. It was another world after all the deprivation we had come to accept. After a few days, 'Bugs' Burrows was detailed to talk on RAF signals procedures to a mass of gum-chewing Yanks and the audience looked a critical bunch and it appeared to be a daunting task for 'Bugs'—we didn't envy him one bit. Nevertheless, he tackled the task with confidence and of course having been part of the A.A.S.F. in France during 1939/40 he was able to recount some of his hair-raising experiences which gained the respect of his audience. Come to think of it, he never did impart much information on Signals procedures but the Yanks loved every minute and were more anxious to learn what they could expect when facing the Hun in combat. They were very anxious to get into combat but of course they were going to have to learn some hard lessons and few of them were going to survive their first taste of operational combat.

A week later, after various lectures, it was decided to carry out a cross-country navigational exercise of 12 aircraft in formation at 28,000 ft. We in the RAF had never flown higher than 20,000 ft. An RAF instructor was to be allocated to each aircraft in the formation—regardless of his trade grouping. Take off was planned for 1400 hours for a flight duration of three and a half hours. We consulted the Flying Notice Board and I saw, with some butterflies in the stomach that I was assigned to the lead aircraft captained by a Lt/Colonel Porter. Climbing aboard, I was staggered at the sight of their radio equipment (General Electric Company) and the hurried briefing by the Radio Operator left me none the wiser!

Fitted with our throat microphones and oxygen masks to be operated at 12,000 ft and above, we took off and the 12 aircraft formated quickly and expertly. We were impressed, our own formation flying had left a lot to be desired. It looked a wonderful sight from the lead aircraft. Our route took us up to Scotland, down the Irish Sea and across

Wales, then back to base. At 20,000 ft whilst negotiating the narrow cat-walk in midships, for what ever reason the bomb-bay doors opened. I was petrified as I looked down and I gripped the guide ropes tightly as the wind rushed through the plane. I would not even blink, let alone move until those bomb doors closed. For the Americans, navigating over the U.K. was difficult in that towns and cities tended to join each other—quite different to what they might experience in the U.S.A. After crossing the coast of Wales it became apparent that the Navigator was unsure of his position and I was summoned by the Captain to obtain QDM's (directional bearings) so that the formation could safely reach base. Being in command of all 12 aircraft, he was most concerned that nothing should go wrong on this their first flight. As I was unaccustomed to the American Radio Equipment I asked the U.S. radio operator to tune to the base frequency and then I took over the Morse key to operate the signals procedure to obtain the necessary courses to steer to reach Bovingdon. After three and a quarter hours in flight we came slap bang over the base and the Captain was complimentary in his remarks. On landing, he said that I had averted some embarrassment for his crew and asked if there was anything he could do for me. It was agreed that a Jeep would be made available for us RAF bodies to journey to London whenever we wished. This generosity was beyond belief. A fortnight later we flew again, this time I was with a Captain Alford on a low cross-country flight at 13,000 ft!! A week later, regrettably we were recalled to our RAF bases at Tatenhill and were back to reality again. We made very good friends at Bovingdon and we wished them luck in their future daylight operations against enemy targets. They certainly did know how to look after their personnel, providing all home comforts and of course the entertainment was first-class, with shows provided by many world-known entertainers, including Al Jolson, Bob Hope and Bing Crosby.

Back at Tatenhill, we related our experiences to those

personnel who had not been so fortunate as to be selected for the detachment and their envy was only too apparent.

EIGHT

Back to O.T.U.

A month later our unit was posted to Church Broughton near Derby and the old routine of training flights was resumed.

In October 1942 it was reasonable to suppose that I would be on instructional duties for about nine months, although one could never be sure. Mollie had received notice that she would be recruited for work in a factory, so I made up my mind to bring her near to the camp if I could locate suitable accommodation for us on a 'living-out' basis.

We were recommended to a Mrs. Beattie Wright and she made us very welcome and comfortable. On the nights that I was flying Mollie had at least company and we were happy with our lot. Came the time that Mollie announced her pregnancy but for fear of not being allowed to stay, we withheld the news from Mrs. Wright. However, she became aware later, when Mollie had an accident falling down the stairs. That night as we lay in bed, Mollie started having terrible tummy pains and I had to summon Mrs. Wright and a doctor. Inevitably Mollie suffered a miscarriage and Mrs. Wright identified the baby as a boy. I would dearly have loved a son but I considered it fate that we were deemed to lose him—perhaps my future destiny was an influencing factor. We had to face the future, come what may.

In October 1942 at 27 O.T.U. we converted to Mark III

Wellingtons which were a considerable improvement on the old IC's. By now the operational squadrons were being equipped with four-engine aircraft although the Wellingtons were still operating in strength. The added capacity of the U.S. 8th Air Force was soon to make its impact and the threat of losing the war would dissipate, albeit there was still a long way to go.

Christmas 1942 arrived and I pondered on how I would overcome the food rationing problem on Christmas Day—as I was living off camp and would not therefore partake of the feast within the Mess. A tour of the local farms proved almost negative, the best I could achieve was the tiniest chicken—about the size of a half-starved pigeon. To divide this pitiful thing between four mouths became unthinkable. I shared my problem with a friend in the Mess kitchen, never disclosing how small my bird was. He came up with the answer. It was arranged that he would leave the kitchen window open sufficiently to reveal the plump turkeys that were prepared for Christmas Dinner, I would remove one and replace it with my 'reject' bird. With furtive glances in all directions whilst there appeared to be a never-ending procession of bodies passing by, I took my chance and did the swap. Going out of the camp I sweated profusely and awaited a challenge from the Guard Room. Luck was with me as some other unfortunate was being closely questioned about some misdemeanour—and I was away. When producing the plump succulent bird to Mollie and Mrs. Wright, their mouths fell open at the sight—nothing like it had ever been seen before. Needless to say, we had a super meal! When next I saw my friend in the Mess kitchen, he grabbed me and said, "You never told me that your bird was a sparrow!" It had obviously caused him some embarrassment although there was plenty for the diners and I hadn't deprived anybody. Of course, my friend touched me for a drink on many occasions thereafter, but it had been worth it.

1943 arrived with no signs of an end to the war. 'Bugs' had been posted to Lossiemouth and a letter from Paul Carlyon confirmed that he had been posted back to 214 Squadron again at Stradishall. Paul contacted Ginger, now Navigator Officer at No. 26 O.T.U. with a view to him joining him on 214 Squadron. However the Chief Instructor refused to release Ginger. God works in mysterious ways because Paul was shot down later over the English Channel and did not survive. There but for the grace of God would have gone Ginger!

My instructional duties continued into March 1943 by which time I was becoming bored with O.T.U. life and thinking about a second tour of operations.

NINE

The Second Tour

On 27th March 1943 my old friend and Gunnery Leader, F/Lt. Jackie Blair D.F.M., said that he wanted to introduce me to a F/Lt. Johnnie Sauvage who was looking for an experienced W/Op-A/G to fly with him on a night bombing exercise at Cannock—a range widely used by O.T.U.'s in the Midlands. We were both impressed with each other, and Johnnie was a debonair but competent pilot who hailed from the Seychelles. Two days later, Johnnie approached me with the idea of undertaking a second tour of operations, his idea being to form a crew of experienced instructors who had already completed one tour of operations. I asked myself if this would be fair to Mollie and at the same time I weighed up the possibility of being returned to operations with an unknown crew—probably with no previous operational experience. Johnnie wanted a quick answer so I decided to throw in my lot with him. Jackie Blair too, opted to become our rear gunner and I suddenly felt safer with such in-built experience. A very competent navigator was chosen by Johnnie and so I met 'Hitch' Hitchcock—another Londoner with considerable experience. We now had the nucleus of a crew so it was left to Johnnie to approach the C.F.I. to request a return to an operational squadron. Mollie did not know that I had volunteered, she just thought it was a routine posting after a long stint on instructional duties. She would have to plan to return to London until I could find alternative living-out quarters near my next posting unit.

The C.F.I. reluctantly agreed to our request and the next day saw us posted to Barkston in 5 Group where we were to form a complete crew, picking up a Flight Engineer and Bomb Aimer—thus confirming that we were to fly in a four-engined aircraft. On 5th April 1943 we found ourselves at Wigsley on 1654 C.U. (Conversion Unit) where we saw our first twin-engined Manchesters. The reports of the 'Manchester' were far from complimentary, they were said to be under-powered and did diabolical things in flight. However, we had to convert to Manchesters before graduating to its four-engined counterpart—the Lancaster.

At this point, we met F/Sgt. Bill Waller who hailed from Romford and was to be our Flight Engineer, and P/O Peter Burbridge our new Bomb-Aimer. This was to be their first tour of operational duty. Both were jovial characters, married and had good O.T.U. performances. So, our crew was now almost complete.

Captain and Pilot	—	F/Lt. J. Sauvage	(Johnnie)
Navigator	—	F/O. H. Hitchcock	(Hitch)
Flight Engineer	—	F/Sgt. W. Waller	(Bill)
Bomb Aimer	—	P/O. H. P. Burbridge	(Peter)
Rear Gunner	—	F/Lt. J. Blair	(Jackie)
W.Op/A.G.	—	F/Sgt. E. Wheeler	(Eddie)

A Mid-Upper Gunner would be recruited on the squadron.

After two flights in Manchester 7491, an initial four hours on 'circuits and bumps' (landings) we did a five-hour cross country including bombing at Bassingham Fen. We were unimpressed with the Manchester and thanked our luck that after only nine hours of conversion we were transferred to Lancasters. What a different experience this was. The Lancaster was a beautiful aircraft in all respects and we immediately fell in love with her. Johnnie said her handling was superb and it was great to have four engines—knowing that it would fly equally well on only two. After only four hours of acclimatization on 'circuits and bumps' we were ready to undertake cross-country exercises, high and low level bombing and gunnery, and 'Bullseye' exercises with the defence forces. We had completed 16 hours day flying and 12 hours at night when we were pronounced 'ready' to join an operational squadron. Imagine our delight and excitement when, on 2nd May 1943 we were posted to No. 97 (Straits Settlement) Squadron in No. 8 Pathfinder Group based at Bourn near Cambridge, with Mark III Lancasters under the command of W/Cdr. R. C. Alabaster D.F.C. For the first time, I'd met a C.O. of a Squadron who was not a pilot. Alabaster was a superb Navigator, and apart from being an efficient C.O., he was an absolute gentleman and was most caring for the crews under his command.

Our living quarters at Bourn were pretty spartan but we enjoyed the atmosphere of life on the squadron.

Two days after arriving, we were called for our first operational briefing at Bourn and the adrenalin started flowing again. We had during that morning undergone fighter affiliation with Thunderbolts based at Debden and we were amazed at the manoeuvreability of the Lancaster, and with the fire power of the rear, mid-upper and front turrets we considered that we could face an adversary with greater confidence than ever before.

We filed into briefing at 1700 hours and saw that our target was Dortmund. We drew a gasp when we saw our bomb load totalled 12,000 lbs, comprising a 4,000 lb. 'Cookie', 4—1,000 lb. and 8—500 lb. G.P. bombs. The all-up weight with our considerable fuel load was staggering, and we wondered how we were going to get airborne on the comparatively short runway. At 2130 hours we were aboard Lanc. ED 862 doing our pre-flight checks and then the four engines burst into life. The sense of power as some 20 aircraft taxied in line from dispersal points to the take-off runway was frightening. When one thought of 240,000 lbs of explosives power, line astern and in close proximity it needed only one aircraft to spark off a major disaster. At 2210 hours, the brakes were released and with all available power we surged down the runway and it seemed we would never lift off before we ran out of runway. At long last we were up—just! It appeared as if we were brushing the tree tops and ascent was painfully slow but sure. Hitch called out a course to steer to reach our coastal rendevous with the main force. I tuned the radio (TR 1154/1155) to the Group frequency ready to receive the Command half hourly broadcasts which, in code, would transmit any relevant information as to target alterations, recalls etc. It was vitally important to listen to and log these transmissions as we were committed to radio silence except in the direst emergency. Transmissions from the aircraft would be picked up immediately by the German listening posts and we would give them ample opportunity to have a 'reception' party waiting for us. Over the sea, the gunners tested their guns after making a careful search for other friendly aircraft. This procedure had to be terminated after a time in view of the danger when forces became so concentrated. The gunners were always apprehensive at the thought that their guns would freeze up after flying at 20,000 plus feet—and one normally had only a split second to act if attacked by an enemy fighter. The warmth of the cabin and the constant droning of the four engines had the effect of introducing drowsiness. To keep myself alert in between broadcasts I took a walk, positioned myself in the astro-dome and peered into the blackness of the night—sometimes to see the red hot exhausts of nearby aircraft or the tell-tale vapour trails. Crossing the enemy coast brought the inevitable deep lines of searchlights and accompanying flak—that had not changed after two and a half years—I remembered it well! We got to the target and the Ruhr was solidly defended. It was a new experience for Peter as he took his position in front of his bombsight. After an initial "Bloody hell" he directed Johnny on to the aiming point with his directions of "Left, left, steady" and it seemed an interminable period before he said "Bombs gone." The uplift after release of our full load was very dramatic. After the photo of our bomb plot was taken, Johnny said, "Let's get the hell out of here," and promptly threw the Lanc around the sky to escape the accurate anti-aircraft fire. As I stood in the astro-dome, the sight below was incredible—it seemed a sea of fire and I could imagine the hell being experienced by those poor unfortunates down there. The return flight was uneventful until we switched on our I.F.F. equipment which identified us as a 'friendly' to U.K. defences. Listening in to the broadcast it was evident that the weather was deteriorating. A landing at base was considered out of the question and we were directed to divert to High Ercall. A landing at a strange aerodrome after six hours of tension was not good for morale—we just wanted to get back to our beds and relax. Not so, we had to await our turn for de-briefing, then to follow the Duty Officer to find available sleeping accommodation here, there and everywhere. But at least we had survived the first trip of our second tour safely. As it was Bill's and Peter's first operation ever I don't think they could sleep at all. They both had done their job competently and we were confident that they would prove to be valuable crew members. We flew back to Bourn the next day and found that there was a stand-down from ops., so we all went into Cambridge to celebrate—which we did in fine style. Eventually, when the pubs closed we found ourselves in the Dorothy Ballroom—a seething mass of dancers in many and varied uniforms. The girls appeared to drift towards the air-crew personnel which didn't always please the Army chaps and there were isolated unpleasantries. There was never time to sit out between dances, one was always grabbed by discerning females. What a lovely life!

A week elapsed after our first operation with 97 Squadron before we were briefed to attack Duisburg in the Ruhr. As our rear-gunner, we recruited Sgt. Geoff Wood who had left the comfort and security of his farm in South America to help the country of his birth. A very shy person, Geoff stood about 5ft 4ins and was on the tubby side with bowed legs, one could imagine him in the saddle of a horse ranging his farm. More so as he always wore a lariat around his waist, and we pictured him trying to lasso enemy fighters if they came too near. Jackie Blair reverted to the mid-upper gun position. The flight was in bright moonlight with no cloud and excellent visibility. The target was clearly identified visually which was a rarity. Our total bomb load of 11,000 lbs went down at 2 am and the glow of the fires was seen from 40 miles away. As usual, the flak was intense and accurate but we came away unscathed and landed at base without incident at 0406 hours. We were awakened at 11 am with news that 'ops' were on again that night and an earlier briefing gave the hint of a longer target. Our flight engineer Bill Waller had to withdraw with a real stinker of a cold, flying at 20,000 ft on oxygen would do him no good at all. His deputy had to be Sgt. Ken Fairlie. When we saw that the target was Pilsen in Czechoslovakia, we wished that we all had bad colds! We took off at 2140 hours and we were not due back at base until approx. 5 am next morning.

In the bomb bays we carried a 4,000 lb 'cookie' and six 500 lb G.P. bombs, not inconsiderable for the distance involved. It was bright moonlight again, visibility very good but considerable ground haze. With such conditions, the gunners and lookouts had to be right on their mettle, we must have been so clearly visible to marauding fighters. A cluster of five red T.I.'s (target indicators) went down as we did our bombing run at 13,000 ft and Peter saw our bombs going through the centre of the cluster. A vague glow was seen through the haze as we turned for home. Seven and a half hours after take off we saw the welcome sight of Cambridge and landed safely at Bourn at 0510 hours. By the time we had been de-briefed and devoured our eggs and bacon breakfast it was 9 am, and tired as we were, it was difficult to get a satisfactory sleep. Up again to lunch, we were delighted to learn that we were not required for 'ops' and many 'cat-naps' were taken in the mess before embarking on another affray in Cambridge.

We were then allocated another aircraft ED940 'N' for Nan—and this letter was to see us through the remainder of our operations. Ten days elapsed during which time we did cross-country flights to get acclimatized to the new

AVRO LANCASTER MK 1 PP687

Reproduced by permission of R.A.F. Museum – Charles E. Brown

Drill Training Squad—Cardington June 1939

The Author—AC2 WOP/AG—May 1940

Bombers of the RAF

Armstrong Whitworth Whitley Mk V of No. 102 Squadron operating from Topcliffe, Yorkshire, in the summer of 1941.

Handley Page Halifax Mk. III of No. 640 Squadron operating from Leconfield, Yorks, early 1945.

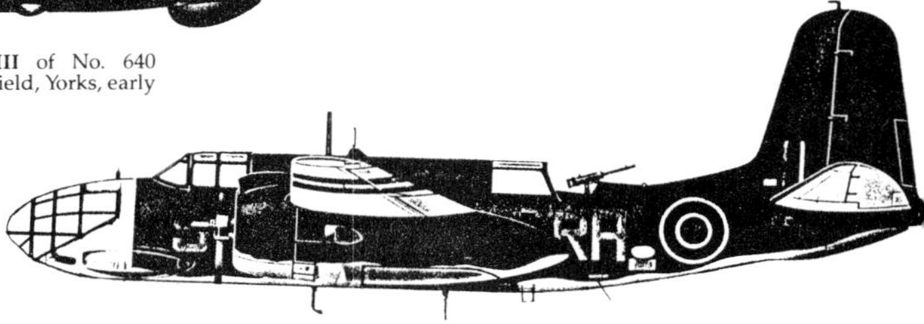

Douglas Boston 111A of No. 88 (Hong Kong) Squadron operating with the 2nd Tactical Air Force flying from Vitry-en-Artois, France, late 1944.

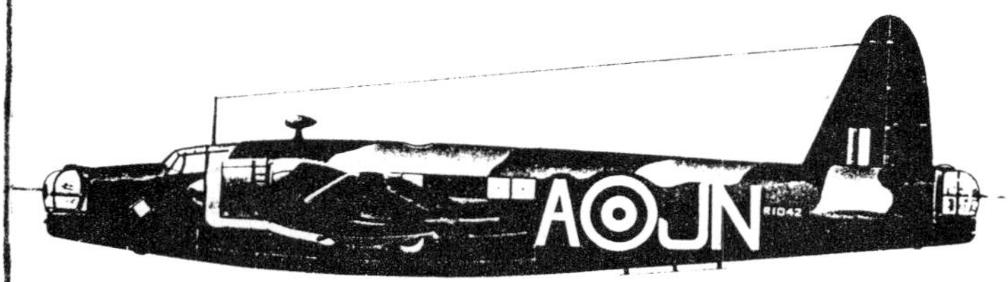

Vickers Wellington Mk. IC of No. 150 Squadron operating from Newton, Notts, winter 1940—41.

De Havilland Mosquito B. Mk. IV of No. 139 Squadron operating from Wyton, Hunts, in the summer of 1943. (This was the second bomber squadron to operate the Mosquito.)

Short Stirling Mk. I of No. 214 Squadron operating from Stradishall, Suffolk, early 1942.

Lockheed Hudson Mk. V maritime patrol aircraft serving with No. 48 Squadron, Coastal Command, in 1941.

Avro Lancaster Mk. I of No. 467 Squadron operating from Waddington, Lincs, spring 1945. This particular aircraft flew 137 operational sorties—the second largest score of any RAF heavy bomber.

Handley Page Hampden Mk. I of No. 44 Squadron operating from Waddington, Lincs, in September 1941.

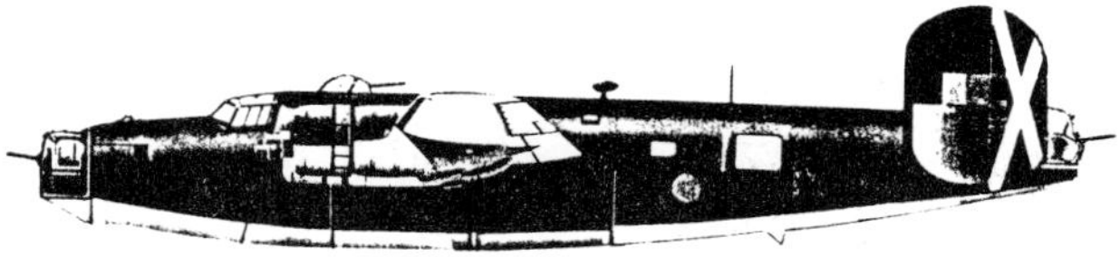

Consolidated Liberator B Mk. VI of No. 356 Squadron operating against the Japanese in the Burma theatre from Salbani, India, early 1945.

Bristol Blenheim Mk. I of No. 60 Squadron based at Lahore, India, during the winter of 1940—41.

Fairey Battle Mk. I light bomber of No. 106 Squadron at Abingdon, Oxon, in August 1938. This unit converted to Hampdens from May 1939.

AUGUST 1941—NEWTON NOTTS

Fred Denman — Eddie Wheeler — Paul Carlyon — Bill Bossom — Ginger Thomas — Sam Huggett

WELLINGTON R1042
December 1940
150 Sq.
Fred 'Denny' Denman   Ed Wheeler   Bill Bossom

Avro Lancaster—All systems 'Go'—Ready for the task ahead

aircraft and then we were back to blitzing the Ruhr once again. These trips of between only four and five hours duration suited us, even if the Ruhr was just about the most heavily defended area of the Reich. We had 'clobbered' Dortmund, Wuppertal and Dusseldorf by the 11th June when we were called by the C.O. W/Cdr. R. C. Alabaster and told that we were to make our first sortie as a Pathfinder Marker. The importance of accuracy in marking the target was emphasised and hundreds of main force aircraft following would be depositing their loads on our marker flares. The target was Bochum. We attacked from 20,000 ft with 5/10ths cloud and at 1.21 am we witnessed one terrific explosion among the many bursts, and fires were taking a good hold. Our first marking raid had been a success and we were elated that our comprehensive training had paid off.

Three days later we were, together with F/Lt. E. Rodley's crew, detailed to R.A.F. Scampton for apparently a special operation. Arriving on 16th June 1943 we found ourselves with detachments of other crews who had been formed into 617 Squadron and had carried out the daring raid on the Mohne and Eder Dams with such devastating success but with high losses. We had to undergo low-level night flying and bombing, and after the dams raid rumours were rife that we would be assigned something similar. We were confined to camp, correspondence and telephone calls being forbidden. There was an air of secrecy about all we did. On 20th June we were called to briefing and looked at each other and said: "Well, this is it. Good luck chaps!"

The target route board was uncovered and we caught our breath as we followed the red route tape down to the bottom of the map and saw no return tape. Then we saw the target—Friedrichshaven Zeppelin Hangars and Workshops which apparently was housing important rocket and radar devices. Straining ourselves to fathom out what was to happen after bombing the target, someone said "We're then flying on to Algiers in North Africa."

The crews hushed as the Station C.O. entered and the

Operations Officer started the briefing. Take off was to be 2145 hours and the total force were to take up loose formation at low level to keep under the enemy radar to create surprise. Crossing the enemy coast, low level was to be maintained until approaching the target area where height was to be increased to 10,000 ft for bombing. In view of the distance involved it would be impossible to return to the U.K. before daylight and the tired force would be easy prey for the fighters that would be amassed and waiting for them. For this reason, the whole formation would then fly on across the Mediterranean to Algiers—landing at Blida or Maison Blanche—subject of course to non-interception by Italian fighters based in Corsica or Sardinia. Return to the U.K. would be via a target in Italy—probably Milan or Turin—a night or two later.

The excitement amongst the crews was intense but certainly it looked a hazardous trip lasting about ten or eleven hours. Our aircraft was to carry mostly target indicators and flares, as was F/Lt. Rodley's aircraft, only two 500 lb bombs being carried additionally. This was to be a real test of our marking ability. We lounged in the Mess writing our last letters to be handed to the Chaplain for forwarding if we did not return. There was an air of nervousness among the crews who were anxious to get on their way.

The buses arrived to take us to our dispersal points. Hitch, our Navigator, turned to me and said: "Ed—I don't bloody fancy this one at all!" I couldn't have agreed more with him. Jackie Blair as usual exuded complete confidence and was already comforting the crew with his anticipations of exploring the Casbah in Algiers. The engines were started and we joined the long procession of aircraft waiting to take off. Ground staff personnel were at the end of the runway to wave us good luck, not knowing the target but anticipating something special—in the wake of the Dam-busting raid. The noise on the ground must have been earsplitting with so many aircraft at such low height. The eyes of the pilots and flight engineers had to be very keen, lifting over trees and high tension wires. As we crossed the enemy coast, it was just like daylight and as we hugged as close to the ground as possible we clearly saw doors of houses thrown open and the occupants waving furiously.

It was an immense feeling of power as we surged on, seeing dozens of aircraft all around us. There had been no flak so far, we were obviously too low and too fast for the light ack-ack but no doubt we were now being plotted even though we had achieved an element of surprise. As we approached Lake Constance for the run-up to Friedrichshaven we climbed to 9,000 ft, Rodley was at 10,000 ft with the main force above us. We clearly identified the target and made our run as the light ack-ack fire came piping up. Peter said how clearly everything stood out and we just beat Ernie Rodley to dropping our markers on the factory roof. Direct hits were observed as we turned to make a further observation and re-mark as necessary. We then ran into the flak which was becoming more intense and suffered hits which affected our hydraulics, one landing wheel dropped slightly with damage thereto. It was time to go, and Hitch gave a course to Johnny for the next leg across the Med. We purposely lost height, the last thing we wanted now was to encounter fighters—even if they were Italian. Daylight broke and we saw Ernie Rodley's aircraft above and on our starboard beam. As he reduced height to about 1,500 ft there was a blinding flash beneath Ernie's fuselage, then his bomb doors opened and a flaming mass dropped out into the sea below. Unknowingly, he had a hung-up marker flare which had failed to release over the target and as it was fitted with a barometric fuse it automatically ignited below 2,000 ft. Fortunately, the flaming mass had dropped out and the fire in the bomb bay became extinguished. Initially it had been a shock to us witnessing the scene but we were relieved to see him continue on his way. The gunners were more alert than ever now, searching the sky for expected interceptors who no doubt would welcome the sight of such big targets with their tired crews.

To cheers from the whole crew and congratulations to

Hitch for good navigation we crossed the North African coast and sighted Algiers. We headed for the airfield at Blida and were re-directed to Maison Blanche where we saw masses of aircraft circling and waiting landing directions. All the planes were now perilously low on fuel, their crews tired, and just anxious to land. The Flying Controller was an American who must have been non-plussed at the sight of so many Lancasters—all calling for permission to land. The first time we heard him he said: "The next baby on the circuit come in and land!" whereupon several anxious pilots headed their aircraft down and it was only too evident that this was a dangerous procedure with more than a likelihood of collisions. The airfield was of sand and stone so clouds of dust rose as an aircraft landed. In spite of exhaustion after being in the air for over ten hours the sequence of landings took a reasonable course. Bill Waller called to Johnny "Fuel almost gone Skipper—we must get down!" Calling the Flying Controller, Johnny reported: "Fuel very low and we have no hydraulics—shot away, landing gear and flaps and brakes inoperative." We were ordered to wait until all other aircraft were down before attempting our landing, lest we littered the airfield before others could get in. Stooging around when fuel gauges were reading nil is no fun and Johnny said, "We're coming in!"

We could not establish if our landing speed was going to be excessive and with no brakes we had no idea where we would finish up. Not knowing to what extent one landing wheel was damaged, Johnny touched down virtually on one wheel and throttled back and hoped for the best. Eventually the undercarriage collapsed and we spun round in clouds of dust—and we were all out of the plane in a flash. We had made it and we felt great! Air Chief Marshall Tedder greeted us and congratulated everybody on the first 'shuttle' flight. All crews were safe and the only aircraft lost was ours—a complete write-off!

After de-briefing we went to the American Mess Tent where we were told to 'scrounge mess tins and irons' (knives and forks) before we got any food. Having obtained the mess tins we queued for our goodies only to find it was stew, followed by peaches. The sight of the stew overflowing into the segment holding the peaches was too much and we abandoned the meal in disgust. Into an allocated tent, with airforce blue battledress and fur-lined boots, made sleeping most uncomfortable in the ever-increasing heat of the day. We were advised not to venture out of camp in our U.K. flying gear—I must say we did rather stand out against our counterparts in their tropical kit. Some crews did however disregard the advice and ventured into Algiers. That afternoon I decided to have a walk around the airfield, perhaps to find a welcoming PX with an ice-cold beer. I was just passing an administrative building when an American Major emerged and called me to him. Unbelievably, he ordered me to follow him to a room where he proceeded to unlock the door. He then handed me a service pistol which he said was loaded, and on entering the adjoining room I was confronted with two German prisoners-of-war who had apparently survived being shot down the previous day. The U.S. Major then said he was arranging for one of his own men to take over the guard duty within the hour. However, it was four hours before I was relieved during which time the Germans were understandably nervous and contemplating their fate. Neither spoke any English and I could understand no German so it was a boring session for all of us. My orders were to stay with them until relieved and if any attempt was made to escape to shoot without hesitation. Of the three of us in that room, I don't know who was the more nervous! Having been relieved by a negro Corporal, I returned to my tent determined not to wander around again to fall into the trap of becoming someone's stooge.

During my enforced stay at Maison Blanche, I was totally unaware that my brother Harry was at the nearby airfield at Blida, and I would dearly have loved to meet him as I hadn't seen him for about three years and had no knowledge of what he had been doing. In fact, he was operating as a Wireless Operator/Air Gunner in Wellingtons and then subsequently in four-engined Liberators. I did not learn until long after the war what awful experiences he had undergone in his flying career, culminating after his 27th operation with his being struck off aircrew status with consequent demotion. Missing an operation for what seemed genuine and reasonable circumstances, he was not allowed to attend and give evidence at his own Court of Enquiry and was found 'Guilty as charged'. Sadly, he was stripped of his rank and posted to Malakal, south of Khartoum in the Sudan, undertaking duties as a land-based Wireless Operator. The only redeeming factor was that he survived the war, whereas his crew were posted missing shortly after his departure.

His story is told as a Postscript to this book and is a revelation of how narrow was the difference between life and death in those fateful years.

The bulk of the shuttle force, with the exception of Johnny and Ernie Rodley were called to briefing, the aircraft having been refuelled and bombed up. The force were to return to the U.K. via Italy and the Alps—bombing Turin on the way. Our crew were given the option of splitting up and flying individually within the other returning aircraft, or waiting at Algiers for some other solution. We did not relish the idea of flying as passengers with other unknown crews so we opted to stay. There was no way that our own aircraft could be repaired but Ernie Rodley's Lanc. was to be patched up, albeit it would take about a week. We languished on the airfield for three days, completely bored, so decided to take a chance of going to Algiers. A cooperative U.S. Paymaster let us have some local currency, so resplendent in blue battledress and fur-lined flying boots we hopped into the back of a service vehicle and were on our way.

In our U.K. uniform we were sweating profusely. In Algiers, we inevitably found the nearest bar but the lager beer was warm and uninviting. I found that my gippy-tummy was turning over and over so it became increasingly urgent to find a toilet to relieve the situation. This was not easy and matters got desperate. Eventually I located the dreaded toilet block and was dismayed to find cubicles without doors and with just two footplates in front of a trough. One had to back onto the metal footplates and aim for the trough in the hope that in a half-standing position you would miss your trousers at half-mast. More disconcerting was the sight of the other 'customers' standing at the cubicle entrance watching you and awaiting their turn to perform. Every half-minute or so there would be a loud yell from the far end followed by a cascade of water rushing through the trough. The stench was abominable and one wanted to get out at the double. Toilet paper was conspicuous by its absence and a hurried search of one's pockets for the odd scrap of paper proved mainly abortive. With the trouser legs soaked and risking a further soaking in the next deluge, I couldn't get out quickly enough. Standing in the warm sunlight for two or three minutes soon had the drying out effect by which time one was contemplating a further 'go'. Nobody had suggested before we left the U.K. to take a change of underclothes, so it takes no imagination to understand our embarrassment.

Standing around the dock area which had recently been bombed was another error. We were so conspicuous in our blue battledress and flying boots that two of us were taken into custody by the local police who suspected that we may have been escaping enemy aviators! Explanations were difficult until the red-capped M.P.'s appeared and they warned us not to leave the airfield again without passes and tropical kit. We hung around the flying control tower daily in the hope of 'hitch hiking' back to the U.K. and a week later we were successful in getting a flight to Gibraltar—a flight of two and three quarter hours. It was a great feeling to be saying goodbye to Algiers. There had, in our opinion, been a sad lack of thought for the crews' welfare on this first shuttle raid. The feeding arrangements after a 10½ hour bombing flight were appalling and no account had been taken of the possibility of crews having to stay on in the event of damage to their aircraft. We would not be keen to be involved in any further shuttle raids. Furthermore, there had been no communication whatever with our families as to our whereabouts or whether we had survived the raid until we returned a week later.

After nine hours in Gibraltar which seemed so pleasant after North Africa, during which time we explored the Rock—and more amenable toilets—I purchased a whole branch of bananas which were unheard of then in the U.K. We saw a Lanc. piloted by P/O Hawkins land on the airstrip and we were told that we were returning to Scampton. A night take-off on such a short runway was not exactly our idea of heaven but we made it . . . just! Taking off at 2230 hours, the nine and a quarter hour flight was uneventful and we touched down at Scampton at 0745 hours next morning. As we emerged from the plane, we were greeted by the Station C.O., and when he saw my branch of bananas he said how nice it was that I should think to bring them back. He peeled off six and handed them to me and said the remainder would be sent to the children in a local hospital. I was dumbfounded, but then agreed totally that it was indeed my intention to do just that. I never did taste one banana as even the six I had were entered as prizes in a raffle!

The next day, 27th June 1943, S/Ldr. Leland arrived to take us back to Bourn where we hoped to be granted some leave after our ordeal, but no such luck. We now had to go through the process of acclimatising to a new aircraft. After six days we resumed marking operations, this time against poor old Cologne again. We were allocated Lanc. III EE176—another 'N' for Nan. With no cloud and excellent visibility we bombed at 0140 hours from 20,000 ft releasing our markers and 10,000 lb bomb load which resulted in a huge explosion at 0143 hours. Landing at 0340 hours, we decided on another thrash to Cambridge that evening. I had now completed my 50th operational sortie which was as good a reason as any to celebrate.

We consumed far too much booze and near to closing time I was feeling very tired and found my way to an outside toilet. In the darkness I must have fallen asleep, for how long was anybody's guess. When I finally came to my senses, I found the toilet door was locked and had no choice but to spend the night there. The rest of the lads had obviously believed that I'd had too much to drink and had gone back to base without a further word. Imagine the Licensee's surprise next morning when he unlocked the door! Fortunately it was a non-flying day and I spent most of the day recuperating—swearing never to drink again—at least not until the next time.

Near the village in Bourn there was a windmill owned by George Papworth—a friend of Mollie's Uncle Syd and the thought struck me that it may be a good idea for us to live out there if the old boy was agreeable. Bill (our F/E) suggested that perhaps his wife Ada and he could join us there. I put the idea to Mollie and she agreed to try and make the arrangements. There was no operational activity for a week and having failed to learn the lesson of not succumbing to the evils of drink, I joined the lads again for another session. Once again I tried to meet the needs of nature—but why were the toilets in perpetual darkness? I should have realised as I fumbled in the darkness that all toilets were completely devoid of toilet paper. Then a thorough search of all pockets and eventually I found a piece of paper—totally inadequate but had to suffice. To my horror, on the bus returning to camp, I suddenly realised I had used a ten-shilling note (50p) in the toilet which made it about the most expensive 'go' I had ever had. Friends on the bus erupted in loud guffaws when I told them and said "What an excuse for getting somebody else to pay your fare!" Jackie said that I was not to be trusted in future and he would keep me on a lead on future forays into Cambridge.

On 11th July, briefing saw us making our first sortie against an Italian target, Turin. Everybody was saying how much easier the 'Eyetie' trips would be after the Ruhr. But of course we had to negotiate the Swiss Alps in each direction. Whilst passing through the Alps, the Swiss no doubt wishing to make a point of their neutrality, opened up with their A.A. fire which although far from accurate, was strange since it came down toward us instead of upwards! Visibility was good and the Alps were an awesome sight. Over Turin we came down to 13,000 ft as the flak was haphazard and didn't present the problems we had come to be used to over Germany. With no cloud and clear visibility the target was defined and we took our time to ensure accuracy of bombing. Peter's words were: "Piece of cake!"

The Group broadcast gave us directions to divert to St. Eval in Cornwall on return, no reason for the diversion being given. After nine and a half hours flying, it was 8 am when we landed. By the time de-briefing was over and we had breakfast it was 10 am and we sprawled in armchairs in the Mess until it was time to return to Bourn. Being called to the Adjutant's office, I wondered what I had done wrong but was pleasantly surprised to hear that I had been promoted to Warrant Officer with effect from 1st May 1943. A trip to the Stores saw me kitted out in a super W/O's uniform—so superior to the previous uniform that I felt like a king. The extra pay too was very welcome. In this highest non-commissioned rank I was well satisfied with the progress I had made in four years and did not relish the thought of being commissioned in the lowly rank of Pilot Officer. It was no doubt a matter of ego, as a Warrant Officer one was recognised as having served a fair term of service whereas as a Pilot Officer I could have been seen to have served very little time at all—almost a 'rookie' with little respect and recognition from the 'other' ranks.

The status within the Sergeant's Mess was another important factor in my resisting advice to apply for a commission. It was not as if I was now intent on making the service my long-term career—even if I survived the war—and married life with its commitments prompted me to think about my eventual return to 'civvy street'.

After a welcome pause of two weeks, my fifty-second operation came up, this time to Hamburg on 24th July. Our established crew were now working well together and we had complete understanding and confidence in each other. We resisted the temptation to go sick on the occasions that we were feeling under the weather lest we should lose our position in this crew. The target at Hamburg did not present too many difficulties in that most of the flight was over the sea and therefore we escaped the attentions of the flak that was experienced during overland trips to places like the Ruhr. We took off at 2200 hours with 8,000 lb of bombs plus our target indicators. There was very little cloud but hazy visibility and at 17,000 ft we ran into the inevitable heavy flak, and released our load at 0105 hours. Two minutes later there was the most violent explosion near the aiming point followed by a glow lasting for 40 seconds. This was later confirmed by all the squadron crews at de-briefing. Many large fires and a pall of smoke were visible as we turned away for that journey back across the dreaded North Sea. Six hours after take off, we touched down at Bourn at 4 am, another satisfactory night's work over.

On this raid, first use was made of 'Window', the metallic strips that were to cause such havoc with the German radar devices. The effect was noticeable because searchlights wandered all over the sky and the flak was haphazard.

Ginger was operational again with 156 Squadron and was also on this raid.

Seven days' leave gave me the opportunity to show off my new uniform to the folks back home. Many times I heard the remark, "He's far too young to be a Warrant Officer," and "Five minutes in the R.A.F. and you're given the highest N.C.O. rank!"

On return from leave we found that new Lancaster III's had arrived fitted with H2S—the latest radar device which enabled a picture of ground detail to be illustrated on a screen sited at the navigator's position. This latest device was to be the greatest advance in radar navigation and bombing technique. It meant that regardless of weather conditions, 10/10th cloud, the ground detail could be identified—and therefore no targets could escape our attention. What a dramatic change from the early days of 1939—1941 when everything was based on 'dead reckoning' navigation and so hopelessly out on many occasions.

Our new aircraft JA908—another 'N' for Nan—took us off on a series of cross-country exercises for 'Y' training with our H2S equipment. We were agreeably surprised with the results of our training in the new aircraft and we looked forward to our next operation to put the training into effect. Imagine our delight to learn that we were on our way this time to another Italian target—Milan. As markers for the following main force we carried only one 4,000 lb 'cookie' in addition to our target indicators. At 1.20 am we attacked at only 12,000 ft with no moon or cloud and good visibility. Many fires were seen and one column of smoke rose to 5,000 ft—still visible from the Alps on the return journey. After eight hours flying, we landed safely at Bourn at 5.30 am.

The next night we were stood down but two aircraft were detailed to attack Mannheim and our Navigator Hitchcock was somewhat dismayed to find himself allocated to a crew captained by F/Lt. Eaton-Clarke for this trip. We urged him not to get lost as we now had got used to him and didn't relish the thought of having to pick up a new navigator for the remainder of this operational tour. Fortunately, Hitch survived this one, arriving back at 0440 hours, getting to bed at 0700 hours—to be awakened with the news that we were all operating again that night.

Johnny Sauvage arrived at briefing with the news that he had been promoted to Squadron Leader—another excuse for a party 'thrash'. Only five aircraft had been allocated for the raid on Nuremburg—including a new crew under the captaincy of P/O L. Baker. It was nearly 2200 hours when we took off for this seven and a half hour flight and we waved to Mollie and Ada (Bill's wife) who were standing on the road at the end of the take-off runway. We were all staying at the Windmill on a living-out basis and thoroughly enjoying our social side of life. The remainder of our crew did not consider it wise to have wives living near the base, knowing when we were away on 'ops' of the anxiety they experienced awaiting our return. At 16,000 ft in 10/10ths cloud conditions, the H2S was proving a most valuable asset to our navigation and we bombed on a timed run but all we saw was a red glow below the cloud. Unfortunately, P/O Baker and his crew did not return from this their first mission.

Two nights later we were off again, a return visit to Milan, and Geoff Wood had to cry off this one with a heavy cold and sore throat, so we had a S/Ldr McKinson as our rear gunner. After bombing from 12,000 ft we had an uneventful return and at 5.30 am after over eight hours in the air Bill and I were anxious to get de-briefing over so that we could get back to the Windmill before the girls were out of bed!!

I was delighted to hear from Ginger that he had met Nancy whilst at O.T.U. at Wing and to receive an invite to his wedding on 14th August 1943. Bish was his best friend and rightfully the correct choice to be his 'best man'.

Mollie and I travelled down by train, as I recollect to Esher in Surrey. We shared the carriage with a woman with a small child who was immaculately dressed in white. It was a very warm day and to my horror Mollie produced a bar of milk chocolate for the child who proceeded to clutch it in her hot little hands and tried to find her mouth. In a matter of seconds the smart white dress became a messy brown splodge and I wished that it could have been a corridor train so that I could disappear. Expressing our regrets and apologies to the mother we alighted from the train in a hurry. We couldn't locate the church but finally made our way to the Reception where Ginger, Bish and I, over the inevitable pint recalled the happenings over the months since we left 150 Squadron. Ginger had joined 156 Squadron at Warboys two months previously to commence his second tour of ops.

Nancy was to produce six sons for Ginger and whilst I know he would dearly have loved a daughter, I guess his 'dead reckoning' navigation was sorely at fault, or was his bomb-sight defective?

Sadly, it was to be the last time I saw Bish, he was killed just after the war at Boscombe Down.

On 17th August we were warned that a special target was to be attacked that night, that we would not be allowed off camp during the day and no outside telephone calls would be allowed. At 10 am Johnny said we were off on a cross-country exercise to sharpen up our 'Y' training. Briefing for only three crews was at 1800 hours under a great veil of secrecy. Entering the Operations Room, we anxiously scoured the room for a hint of this 'special' target. The route map was obscured by a sheet until the C.O. arrived. When the unveiling revealed the target, we were none the wiser as it identified Peenemunde—which meant absolutely nothing to any of us—we had never hard of it! The Intelligence Officer rose to give his briefing and said that the target on the Baltic Coast was probably the most important target ever to be attacked. Whilst not revealing it was a site for the development and production of V1 flying bombs and V2 rockets, he said that advanced radar equipment was its main function. Three aiming points, including scientist and production worker billets had to be destroyed totally—if not tonight, then tomorrow night and the night after if necessary. We were told that Peenemunde could alter the whole course of the war and had to be destroyed regardless of losses. This did nothing to encourage us especially when we learnt that there would be no cloud and a full moon, and the attack would be from as low as 12,000 ft or lower. These conditions would be ideal for the German Night Fighters so the R.A.F. would adopt spoof tactics by sending a small number of Mosquitoes to Berlin, giving the impression that that was the night's target for the main force. Much publicity had been given to the fact that Berlin was high on the R.A.F. priority list and the

Germans were very sensitive to attacks on their capital city. It was hoped that their fighters would be concentrated nearer to Berlin and that by the time it was established that Peenemunde was to be the main target, the first two waves of bombers would have completed their task and been on the way home. The third wave—provided by No. 5 Group—could however expect to have a hot time. We took off at 2108 hours and climbed to 18,000 ft—our primary target was the scientist's quarters. The whole force would be directed by a Master Bomber—G/Capt. John Searby of 83 Squadron based at Wyton was selected for this task—and he was to fly over the target for the whole attack giving a commentary and shifting the attack as was necessary. Forty minutes would elapse from first to last aircraft on target. Some aircraft were fitted with 'OBOE'—ground controlled radar—other PFF aircraft with H2S, but the conditions would allow for full visual attacks providing smoke did not obscure the aiming points. From 08°E we started to throw out 'Window'. We began to lose height as we approached Rugen Island and saw many aircraft around us in the almost daylight conditions. Fortunately none were hostile so hopefully the Mosquitoes who had preceded us by one hour had lured the night fighters to the Berlin area. We sighted the target clearly at 11,700 ft and already a smoke screen had been started by the enemy in the hope of thwarting the attacking forces. Light flak started piping up from the target zone as we went in with our green T.I.'s and 7,500 lb bomb load. Peter reported direct hits on the living quarters and just then we suffered a direct hit from flak. Johnny shouted that we were going round in circles and could not fly straight and level. If the state of affairs could not be rectified we would have to consider bailing out—a prospect which did not appeal one bit. To jump with the possibility of either landing in the sea or amid a hail of bombs just wasn't on.

Bill beckoned me to follow him down the fuselage and with great trepidation I did so, regretting the fact that I was putting distance between me and my parachute. Bill indicated the trimming and aileron cables that had been severed by the impact. He busied himself with lengths of nylon cord and then Johnny said that he had recovered control of the aircraft. By now the target was a sea of flame and high explosions, and we were intent on returning from whence we came with all speed. The German defences were well alerted by now and fighters would be re-deployed from the Berlin area without delay. We felt sorry for the last wave of bombers entering the scene who would have to take the full brunt of attacks in ideal night-flying conditions. Several aircraft were seen going down in flames. Seven hours after take-off we had the welcoming sight of Bourn and we hoped that the target had been well and truly plastered and that it would not be necessary to return again the next night, when the Luftwaffe would be ready and waiting to wreak their revenge. Initial reports that morning indicated that the raid had been a complete success achieved through the element of surprise, the decoy raid on Berlin and the sheer audacity of operating under a full moon and clear skies. Out of the total of 606 aircraft assigned, 40 four-engined bombers and one Mosquito were lost (6.7%) and 32 suffered damage. In the daylight reconnaisance 12 hours after the attack, photographs revealed 27 buildings in the northern manuacturing area destroyed and 40 huts in the living and sleeping quarters completely flattened. The foreign labour camp to the south suffered worst of all. The whole target area was covered in craters. It was inconceivable that the site could ever operate again and at least we had gained valuable time against V1 and V2 attacks on London and our impending second front assault forces. This raid probably gave us our most satisfaction against all other targets attacked.

Ginger had been excused this operation, having better things to do as he was on his honeymoon. The morning after the raid, other guests in the hotel asked him where Peenemunde was and he became an embarrassed Pathfinder when he was unable to tell them.

We were all now displaying our Pathfinder Force badges

with pride, having completed our tests and the necessary operational experience. I recalled my first test by the then G/Capt. Donald Bennett himself. He personally tested me with morse transmissions and receiving, questioned me on various aspects of gunnery, then beckoned me to a wall chart of stars. He pointed to a particular star and asked me to identify it. In my hesitation to work my way round from the North Star, he shifted irritably and then said: "You're no good to me if you don't know your stars. Come back again when you have the right knowledge!" Several weeks later I went for my second test, confident that I could identify any group of stars, but this time he never posed a question on the stars and I was granted my certificate confirming the award of the Permanent Pathfinder Badge.

Twenty third August 1943 saw us making our first assault against the capital city—Berlin—always considered to be the 'big one'. It meant a long trip over heavily defended enemy territory and the Berlin defences were savage in the protection of the great city which the Nazis had sworn would never be subjected to air bombardment. What a long way I had come since those dark days in 1940 when there appeared to be no salvation from the gloom, and here we were attacking the German capital in strength and talking more and more of an invasion of Europe. This was to be my 57th operation, could I survive to see that 60th operation? It did seem to be inviting the inevitable with each further raid, so many crews had not even reached double figures, and with so many more aircraft involved, losses mounted so that the likelihood of aircrews surviving 12 raids was still minimal. For this trip, we had an additional crew member—a F/Sgt. Penny who came as second pilot for the experience. Apart from the heavy flak and searchlight activity, the flight was uneventful, far less frightening than any trip to the Ruhr, and after bombing from 18,000 ft we were back at base in 6 hours 35 minutes.

Four nights later we were back to Nuremburg with another 7,000 lbs of 'goodies'. These were placed on workshops and marshalling yards, bombing with the aid of H2S.

On return we were coned by searchlights and suddenly the heavy flak stopped which indicated fighter activity could be expected. Jacky in the mid-upper turret spotted a fighter attacking from the starboard quarter and gave Johnny instructions to 'corkscrew' and he and Geoff in the rear turret gave a burst of fire which made 'N' for Nan shudder, and the smell of cordite in the cabin was pungent. I was sitting at my radio listening to the Group broadcast and as I looked up I saw that there was a clean hole through the crystal monitor about eighteen inches above and to the right of my head. A cannon shell had pierced it and gone straight out through the front of the aircraft. I was rigid, not daring to move an inch. The contact was brief and the fighter sheered off—much to our relief. One of the crews, captained by F/Lt. C. B. Robertson, did not return from this operation.

On 31st August, our hearts dropped again when we saw that the target was again Berlin, it seemed that the targets were becoming so much harder these days and I gained the impression that time was running out for me and the odds were ever-increasing. It was at this stage that I was becoming more nervous then ever before and was looking forward to finishing my tour of ops. Although we had a satisfactory trip we were upset to hear that W/Cdr. Burns had been shot down, it being subsequently established that the crew had been taken Prisoners of War, except for F/O Dolby who had been killed.

The raids on Berlin were becoming monotonous when we found ourselves in flight again on September 3rd against the 'Big City'. The seven and a half hour return trip was carried out without too much trouble. There was no moon, no cloud and good visibility, and our bombs released from 19,000 ft were seen to burst in a built up area. The flak as usual was intense and accurate but we escaped damage. From the frequency of raids on the Capital City, it was only too evident that the 'Battle of Berlin' had started in earnest and we were repaying ten-fold the attacks on London in 1940/41. All our crews returned from this operation, one having to return early after two hours when Sgt. Miller's mid-upper Gunner Sgt. Williams was rendered unconscious at 20,000 ft after his electrically heated suit and oxygen supply failed.

The next night was a stand down for the squadron but then two nights running, on the 5th and 6th September we were to attack Mannheim and Munich.

On the Mannheim trip, a crew had to abandon this mission for the second consecutive night, this time as a result of the rear turret elevation and depression being unserviceable. I cannot recall ever seeing that crew again at subsequent briefings.

The Allies were doing well at this stage of the war. Italy having been invaded, had surrendered—obviously to the disgust of the Germans who were still strongly resisting the push to the North. On the Eastern front, the Russians had begun to regain ground after having been pushed back to the gates of Moscow.

My 63rd operation, on 22nd September, was against Hanover, the birthplace of my great-grandfather. The following night it was Mannheim, and it was on this operation that we lost F/Lt. Fletcher and crew, including W/O Layne the Wireless Operator who was on his second tour of 'ops' and was never to learn that he had been awarded a D.F.C. for earlier raids. The loss of this most experienced crew made me wonder how much longer our luck could hold out. I had exceeded 60 ops and wondered how soon I could be relieved. It was to be just one more week before my operational career was to come to an end, but in that week I was to fly to Mannheim, again, to Brunswick and finally to Munich. On the Mannheim raid, we were coned by searchlights for a whole six minutes; it seemed as if every flak battery was concentrating on us and I thought it would be only a matter of seconds before they scored a direct hit. After a battering during this interminable period during which I had virtually given up any hope of escaping, Johnny finally gave them the slip by violent evasive action and we were away and on the return flight.

If ever I prayed, it was never more earnestly than on that night.

Setting out for Munich, on the night of 2nd October 1943, we had no prior knowledge that this would be our final operation together. Perhaps it was just as well as we might have been even more nervous in our anxiety to survive. As it was, the trip was largely uneventful except that we coaxed Hitch our Navigator to leave his seat and take up position in the astro-dome to see what was going on over the target area. His remarks over the inter-com brought smiles to our faces when he said, "Christ! Does this sort of thing go on every night?" Seeing the target area a mass of fires he considered it was "sheer bloody murder." Ginger too was on this raid and he was to be involved in five further operations against Berlin.

Our crew was stood down for a few days after this until Johnny called us together and said, "Well lads, do we want to go on, or for some of us at least, shall we call it a day?" For Johnny, Hitch, Jackie Blair and myself—we had done our quota and would ask to be relieved of further operational duty. For the other chaps, Bill (F/E), Peter (A/B) and Geoff (R/G) they had no option but to continue. Peter anxiously cleaned his pipe, Bill kept shuffling his feet and Geoff nervously fingered his lanyard whilst the rest of us tried to reach a decision. If we old-stagers decided to finish, then Bill, Peter and Geoff would be assigned to a new crew to finish their first tour. Whilst they were hopeful that the crew would not split up, they recognised that we had done our fair share of ops over a long period and in similar circumstances they would say "enough is enough." Johnny posed the question to us again and there seemed a reluctance to reply. Finally, I said that the last half dozen trips had been a nightmare for me and I had been getting progressively more nervous, so I was going to call it a day. Hitch, too, said he agreed with me and so it was decided to tell the C.O. W/Cdr. Alabaster that we had made up our minds. Naturally, the other three lads were disappointed, but they thanked us for the happy times we had enjoyed at Bourn, and we wished them all the luck that was going.

We were to remain at Bourn for a further three weeks before learning of our postings, but two of these were spent on leave. It was whilst I was at home on leave that I learned from the Islington Gazette that I was awarded the D.F.C. it being announced in the London Gazette on 19th October 1943. My joy was complete, I had survived 66 operations, three others didn't count due to aborts, I had been decorated, my official Permanent Pathfinder Certificate had arrived, many new aircrews were arriving daily to take up the challenge where I left off, and now I could more hopefully expect to see the end of the war and carry on with my happily married life. During this leave, I was invited to visit the Company I had worked for prior to the war—Herbert & Sons Ltd., at their Edmonton premises. The reception was overwhelming. The entire workforce were assembled and after a speech by my old friend Stan Kitchen, I stepped forward to receive from the Scale Shop Foreman, Fred Pennell, a beautiful barometer suitably inscribed: "To mark the occasion on the award of a D.F.C." I was choked for words. My world was complete, the good Lord had looked kindly on me and protected me through four hard years of war during which so many thousands had died. Proudly wearing the mauve and white ribbon alongside that of the 1939/43 Star, I returned to Bourn to receive the congratulations of the rest of the crew, and was delighted to find that Johnny and Hitch had also been decorated. I was saddened then to hear the news that Paul Carlyon, with whom I had flown in 1940/41, had been shot down and killed over the Bay of Biscay in a raid on Lorient some months earlier. News filtered through fast at this time and I learned that Fred Denman, my friend and front gunner on Wellingtons had been decorated with the D.F.M. out in the Middle East where he completed his second tour—again on Wellingtons.

* * * * *

Before I leave behind this period of operational duty, it might interest my readers to know something about the 'ordinary', day-to-day routine which had become our way of life.

The term 'uneventful' quoted against many of the sorties described during two tours of operational duty were deemed so only because of the fact that we did not encounter fighter attacks or sustain major damage from anti-aircraft fire from the ground defences.

There were still many dangers from adverse weather conditions, severe icing, mechanical problems, and navigational errors prior to the advent of radar aids, all of which constituted normally acceptable flying hazards.

A typical 'uneventful' raid experienced by crews would, by today's standards, be considered anything but uneventful!

A day on an operational bomber squadron would begin when brought to readiness by Group H.Q.'s teleprinter message that operations were 'on' for that night, and there would be noticeable activity throughout the Station. Ground crews, encompassing all trades, would swarm around the aircraft to bring them to full operational standard. Engine and air-frame fitters carrying out their inspections and tests, wireless and electrical engineers checking their equipment and changing batteries, armourers replenishing ammunition, checking rotation of turrets, installing bomb-sights, instrument technicians testing and checking dials and instruments, oxygen bottles being replaced, each aircraft was a hive of industry. All were under the watchful eye of the Engineering N.C.O. in charge who was responsible for reporting to the Captain of aircraft that all was in order.

The loading of fuel and the bomb-load would be the last task, this being dependent on the target and distance involved.

The air-crew would then undertake an air-test, usually taking about twenty minutes or so. On landing, the Captain would be presented with Form 700 for signature to confirm acceptance of the aircraft's serviceability, or he would advise the Chief Engineer of any faults needing to be rectified. The aircrew would then disperse to relax prior to being called for briefing. On many occasions, the crews would be 'stood down' and they would heave sighs of relief that at least they would survive one further night.

However, when it was 'all systems go', Group HQ would send by teleprinter details of aircraft required, the target, route to be taken in both directions, bomb loads and any relevant information, whereupon the Squadron Navigation Leader would plot the flight, determine the fuel load, times of take-off to reach the target at the time specified by Group, and list possible diversion aerodromes in the event of adverse weather conditions prevailing at base on return.

Operation briefing time would be communicated to the Officers' and Sergeant's Messes together with times of pre-flight meals. In-flight rations and flasks of coffee would be prepared.

Late activity on the airfield would see the huge petrol bowsers moving from one aircraft to the next, and long trailers hauling their bomb loads from the bomb-dump to dispersal points with gangs of armourers waiting to winch them into the aircraft bomb-bays. It was fascinating to watch the efficiency with which these lads fitted nose and tail fuzes and then winched the bombs, sometimes up to 12,000 lbs, into position, then moving on to the next plane.

Aircrews would be relaxing in many ways before briefing, some playing cards, snooker or darts, others quietly reading or writing letters, and some just staring into space.

Came the time to attend briefing, the Operations Room was a hubbub of noise until the Squadron Commander entered, followed by his specialist Officers, when everybody sprang to attention. Waved down by the C.O., the cloth that covered the target map would be removed. Some targets were better received than others, Berlin for instance drew groans from the crews, whereas Italian trips brought little reaction. The heavily defended Ruhr area was always dreaded.

Each specialist Officer spoke on his particular aspect of the operation, after which the C.O. would invite: "Any questions?" Then he would wish us luck and leave.

Navigators and Captains would remain behind to plot their courses on the maps, noting heavily defended areas en route and any special instructions. The other crew members withdrew to their various Section leaders for their instructions. The Wireless Operator would be issued with the VERY cartridges for the colours of the day, to be fired off if challenged by friendly fighters or ack-ack defences. He would also be advised of radio frequencies to be used and enemy radio beacons that could assist our navigation.

Bomb-aimers would be instructed as to the strategy to be adopted in reaching their aiming points, and Gunners advised as to whether and when they could test their guns in flight, tactics to be adopted against fighter interception.

The dining halls were a hubbub of conversation as the pre-flight meal was served. Many were the times you would hear, "Can I have your eggs and bacon if you don't come back?" Many flippant remarks disguised the nervousness among crews prior to take-off, but once in the air this tended to disappear once fully engaged with the task in hand.

The crew rooms were a hive of activity as gunners donned their heavy electrically heated suits, flying boots were pulled on, parachute harnesses put on over voluminous coverings of warm clothing and Mae Wests, helmets and oxygen masks examined. Navigators with their hold-alls carrying maps, charts and sextant, Wireless Operators with their code books and radio frequency tables, Gunners carrying the coffee flasks and packets of confectionery comprising chocolate and fruit sweets, and cans of orange juice, would all troop out to the waiting transport to take them to their aircraft out on the far dispersal areas. Jocular remarks were made by one crew to another and the inevitable two-finger signs were predominant.

At dispersal, the faithful ground-crews were waiting to

give a helping hand to the aircrews boarding the plane and then standing by the starter motors until starting-up time was signalled by the Captain. The first engines would burst into life and one by one the others would follow until the air was filled with the roar of possibly 20 or so aircraft. After run-up, chocks were removed from the wheels, and the long procession of aircraft would move out on the perimeter track to take up their position at the end of the runway. With maximum load, great care had to be exercised in keeping the plane on the concrete perimeter, running off onto the softer grassy areas could so easily have caused an aircraft to become bogged down and consequently abort the take-off of those taxiing behind.

Radio silence was maintained to prevent the enemy's listening posts gaining prior knowledge of an impending attack, and take-off was indicated by a green Aldis Lamp flashed from the Air Traffic Control caravan sited by the side of the runway.

Facing into the wind, the Captain would call for "full boost" and then, releasing the brakes, the aircraft would gather increasing speed nose-down to lift off it's massive load just before the end of the runway. The impression was that we were not going to clear the trees at the airfield perimeter. Fortunately we always did, and we would all-so-slowly gather height before setting course on the first leg of the route out.

The Navigator would call "first course 090 degrees" or whatever, and the compass would be set accordingly. As soon as sufficient height was gained the Wireless Operator proceeded to the rear of the plane to let out the trailing aerial to gain maximum radio signal strength. In the case of four-engined aircraft, the Flight Engineer ensured that the landing wheels were securely locked up after take-off and would then check the instrument panels to ensure that all systems were functioning satisfactorily. The gunners would be on full alert against possible enemy intruders, there was never really a time to relax.

Climbing through cloud with such volume of aircraft

involved was always hazardous and a sharp look-out was vital.

The bomb-aimer and rear gunner would co-operate with the Navigator in determining wind drifts, the Wireless Op. would keep a listening-out watch on the Group frequency and the Pilot would adhere to the pre-determined height and speeds to reach the target at the right time.

As we approached the enemy coast, an even fuller alert was necessary as interceptions and engagements with enemy fighters tended to be all over within seconds. Over the coastline, invariably searchlights would begin their probing, and near to sensitive and defended areas the flak would start bursting around the aircraft. Puffs of black smoke would be seen and the crump of bursting shells heard above the noise of the engines. The Pilot would maintain his course and speed unless the situation became untenable and he was forced to vary his height and speed. Guns would have been switched from 'safe' to 'fire' in readiness for any attack.

The Navigator would fix his position from time to time by use of his 'Gee' radar set, in earlier times when radar assistance was not available he would use his sextant for this purpose, providing the stars were visible. Help was on occasions forthcoming from the W/Op. when D/F loop bearings were obtained from enemy radio beacons.

On occasions, dependent on the target, searchlight belts up to 50 miles in depth would be encountered and it seemed that the plane was perpetually illuminated, which was quite frightening.

Approaching the target area, the bomb-aimer took up his position in the nose of the aircraft and checked his bomb-sight and the fuse switches on the master panel. The Wireless Op. went into the astro-dome position to provide another pair of eyes. Other friendly aircraft would probably be sighted above, below or on either side.

Timing of an attack was all-important, one did not wish to arrive too early with the prospect of having to go round again. The flight engineer would cast a critical eye on the fuel gauges and there would be great tension until the considerable bomb loads were released. Varying amounts of damage could be sustained en route to the target without drastically affecting the efficiency of the flight, nevertheless this could be very perplexing. The excitement had a distinct effect on the bowels at times and a tightening of stomach muscles always seemed prevalent.

The run-up to bomb release appeared interminable, with the bomb-aimer calling for "Bomb doors open" and the Captain's response, then a lengthy "Right, right, steady"—a pregnant pause, final directional adjustments until you heard the magic words "Bombs gone!" With flak bursting around, a direct hit could be the end!

In front of the radio set, I had a bucket seat in which I placed my parachute to give me more height to see the dials, and on occasions it was very difficult to remove it. I used to ponder on this problem during our run-up to the target and often felt uneasy about the time factor should I need to leave the aircraft in a hurry. The rear gunner too had a problem as there was insufficient space in the turret to store his 'chute, and he stacked it in the main fuselage near his turret doors. The turret door locks were known to be suspect on occasions—some gunners were sucked out when the doors burst open on full rotation of the turret. In one attack on a squadron aircraft, the rear guns jammed and in the heat of the moment the gunner unwittingly removed his heated gloves to clear the blockage but as soon as he touched the bare metal his skin became welded to it and he consequently suffered severe frostbite.

Once having released the bombs, the aimer would check to establish that all had gone and that there were no hang-ups to cause further problems. The Pilot would then leave the target area at speed to evade the defences and turn on to a course given by the Navigator.

Many occasions saw encounters by other aircraft with enemy fighters, and plots were made and times noted of aircraft destroyed or seen to be going down.

Calculations were made of remaining fuel to ensure

economical use on the return flight in order to reach base safely. Encounters with enemy fighters could create long diversions with the danger of using up precious fuel and thus failing to achieve landfall and having to face a possible ditching in the North Sea. That prospect gave little hope of survival.

Parched throats were relieved by the hot coffee in our flasks, which was usually drunk somewhere on the homeward run when things seemed quiet. In the sometimes excessive heat of the cabin, or in the extreme cold if the heating failed, the coffee was a welcome relief. It was a great feeling just to unbutton the rubbery oxygen mask for a minute or so.

When nature called, a journey was made in the darkness to the Elsan toilet located behind the main spar but all gun positions had to be covered by the Wireless Op. or Flight Engineer until the gunners returned. The Pilot was not so lucky and had to use a bottle or tin which proved difficult when one hand remained on the controls. Many the curses when their aim was not accurate!

Crossing the enemy coast was no guarantee of safety. Flak ships would give a sharp reminder of their presence, and of course there were the marauding fighters anxious to wreak their havoc on unsuspecting crews. Nearing the home coast, the Wireless Op. would switch on the IFF apparatus to identify us as a 'friendly' to the UK defences. However, there were many trigger-happy naval types who were taking no chances, banging away at anything in the air causing us to fire off the colours of the day.

Without relaxing fully, it was a relief to make landfall, and we hoped that weather conditions at base were favourable and that there was no intruder alarm in force. A radio listening-out brief was maintained and we groaned whenever we were diverted to another station. We only looked forward to our own beds.

All the crew kept an eye out for the flashing beacon to identify their own airfield. There were many flashing due to the close proximity of the 'dromes in East Anglia, but when none were flashing it was evident that German night intruders were about.

Only if the Navigator had serious doubts about his position would he ask the radio operator to break silence and obtain QDM's (homing bearings) to reach base, there being the risk that such transmission would be homed onto by a night fighter.

Having identified base, the Wireless Op. would have to remember to wind-in his trailing aerial, as failure to do so could be lethal to the flarepath crew when landing. The Pilot would call up the Controller on R/T for permission to land and there could be say 20 aircraft in the circuit, some short of fuel or damaged. The planes would have to be given staggered flying heights to avoid collisions, and an order in which to land. Eventually we would make our final approach, say a small prayer that we would land safely, and with the screech of the tyres on the runway we would congratulate ourselves on having completed one more operation. Thoughts would then move on to other crews, hoping they had been as fortunate as we were.

With the aid of torches, the ground crews would guide us into our parking spots, the engines would be switched off and chocks placed in front of the main wheels. With final checks to ensure all equipment was switched off, we would descend onto the tarmac to be warmly greeted by our ground crew who were on first name terms. They would be anxious to know if we had experienced any problems with the aircraft or equipment, or whether we had sustained any damage. The smokers among the crew would light up their cigarettes, take a first lengthy draw and make comments on how they thought the flight had gone.

Within minutes the aircrew 'bus, invariably driven by a pretty WAAF would arrive to take us back to the Operations Block for de-briefing by the Intelligence Staff who had probably been sitting around for hours awaiting our return. We would be greeted by the C.O. and the Chaplain who would be first to offer us a cup of tea or coffee and biscuits, asking if all was well with us. Signs of weariness showed on the faces of all crew members whether the flight duration had been four or ten hours.

Intelligence Officers would ply their questions concerning the defences both en route and return, all aspects of the raid, combats, time of bombing and observed results, time and position of aircraft seen destroyed or going down, weather conditions at all stages, how radar worked etc. etc. The logs were handed over to the Navigation and Signals Leaders, whereupon we would take a last look at the Operations Board to see who had not yet returned. There were sometimes some comments like 'Mayday' signals heard. Off to the Crew Rooms then to discard flying clothing, parachutes and harnesses, then back to the Officers' or Sergeants' Messes for our usual eggs and bacon breakfast. Whilst hungrily consuming this meal, the crews would talk about their own particular experiences. Some would then wait in the Mess for absent friends, others would be away to bed, wondering if the experience was to be repeated again that night.

Such was an 'uneventful' trip!

Many a time the dreaded foggy conditions prevailed at base on return, and it was sickening that so many aircraft would crash with the loss of all crew members after reaching and returning from a target. When fog was dense and it was senseless to attempt a landing, we would be diverted to an aerodrome equipped with F.I.D.O. On such bases, for example at Ludford Magna, petrol pipes ran the length of a runway and would be ignited to disperse the fog, and flames would reach a height of about six feet or so. It would illuminate the runway satisfactorily but it was always frightening as you touched down, it seemed that you were flying into intense flames. Nevertheless, it was preferred to making almost blind landings and was no doubt instrumental in saving the lives of many aircrew.

It was strange how crews related to their own particular aircraft and they were never so confident on the occasions that they had to use an alternative machine, for whatever reasons. Even the smells in their aircraft could be identified, strange as that may seem.

On the subject of smells, these were very dominant, particularly in the heat of battle. There was the combination emanating from the heating system, creating body odours, the smell from the dope covering various patches of the fuselage from previous damage, the strong pungent cordite smells when one had experienced a heavy flak barrage or after the plane's guns had been fired. Additionally, there was a constant smell of fear about the aircraft during flight, emphasised by the odd trips to the Elsan toilet. The rubber oxygen mask too created its problems with the sweat and condensation.

After landing, the crew would delight in taking great gulps of fresh air, even if some then proceeded to light up cigarettes to relax jaded nerves. The sweetest smell of all was when one entered the Mess after de-briefing to that marvellous aroma of fried bacon and coffee. Or was it the realisation that one was a survivor?

PART III

TEN

Operations Completed

On 27th October 1943, my posting had come through, I was to proceed to No. 18 O.T.U. at Finningley in Yorkshire for a second bout of flying instructional duties. I was not to know where Johnny, Hitch or Jackie were to be posted or what was to happen to them until after the war. One other posting to the O.T.U. from 97 Squadron was W/O S. C. Bremner D.F.C., a Navigator who had completed two tours of ops.

I was not long at Finningley before I found myself detached to Worksop where I made good friends with W/O Eddie Wain D.F.M., a Wireless Operator who hailed from Bradford. Once again I found myself embroiled in the hazards of flying with pupil crews on cross-country, bombing and gunnery exercises. Well, I thought, it perhaps was better than having all that flak thrown at you, and the prospects of having to swim the North Sea!

I decided that I would like to live out of camp again and Mollie was in favour. It was on the cards that I would stay at Worksop for probably a year at least. Not far from the air base, there was a huge camp occupied by the Rifle Brigade at Ranby, which was not far from Retford, and the C.O. there was apparently David Niven the film actor. My search around the villages on bicycle brought me to the Gate Inn at Ordsall near Retford where I decided to have a pint and a sandwich. The Landlady, Mrs. Carrie Willis, was a jolly, generous type probably in her early 50s and we struck up an immediate friendship. I told her that I was trying to find accommodation for my wife and myself, that I was anxious to get Mollie away from the bombing in London. She said that she did have some limited accommodation herself in the Gate Inn and that she charged normally 9/6d. (48p) a day bed and breakfast and 3/6d. (18p) for an evening meal. A swift calculation soon scotched any idea of my being able to afford those prices even with the living-out allowance from the R.A.F. I made a few visits on the evenings I wasn't flying and Mrs. Willis came over to me one night and brought me a pint with her compliments. She had been thinking about my problem and thought she could help after all. For 50 shillings (£2.50) a week, we could have a double room and an evening meal there, and I thanked her for her generous offer. I couldn't wait to write to Mollie and arrange for her to come and see the Gate Inn. The room was super, with a lovely double bed, and we could have the run of the pub. We agreed to accept the offer until something else came up and so we were ensconced in Ordsall. I could cycle to the camp within half an hour and so we were delighted to be together at last. We thoroughly enjoyed our stay there, the food was superb and of course I could get a drink whenever I wished, in spite of the licensing laws!

Living off camp was a sheer delight and whilst the Gate Inn was home from home, it was evident that I had to locate cheaper lodgings. It was through Bert Pike—a member of the Rifle Brigade—and his wife Iris, that we were to be introduced to a Mr. and Mrs. Truswell who provided our living-out accommodation for the next year. I could cycle to the aerodrome from Retford in half an hour, the accommodation was excellent, and the Truswells were a nice couple with two young sons, Alan and Jack. Bert and Iris came from East Ham in London and we were to form a strong bond of friendship with them which has lasted to the present day.

I had been at Worksop just a few weeks when I heard some very sad news. Bill Waller and Peter Burbridge had entered a new crew after our departure from 97 Squadron at Bourn and had completed only four more operations when they were reported missing after a raid on Berlin. It subsequently transpired that their aircraft had received a direct hit on their bombing run and had exploded with its full bomb load. They wouldn't have known anything about it. Peter's wife had only recently given birth to twins, and Bill's wife Ada would have been devastated as she was totally devoted to him. I felt sick for days after that news, feeling perhaps that they might have lived if our original crew had continued. On the other hand, we too may have died on that fateful Berlin raid—who knows?

It wasn't until long after the war that I learned that Ginger Thomas was with 156 Squadron at Warboys at about the time I was at Bourn. Furthermore, as I left 97 Squadron, 'Rocky' Belleroche (ex Battles/Wellingtons of 150 Squadron 1940/41) arrived there to carry out his further tour of operations. Rocky was over Darmstadt when his Lancaster sustained a direct hit and the aircraft broke up. He found himself alone in the cockpit section of the plane, finally freed himself and baled out. He damaged his back on landing in a garden with his 'chute draped over a wall. The inhabitants were evidently in an air-raid shelter. Because of his injuries he was unable to evade capture and spent the rest of the war in a P.O.W. camp, finally overrun by the Russians. Ginger completed his second tour, reaching 60 operations in total, received a D.S.O. in addition to his D.F.M. and was then posted to H.Q. Bomber Command where he worked under Air Chief Marshal 'Bomber' Harris. The three of us could say that we had earned our keep since those days back in 1939—40. And we lived to meet up again over 40 years after the war!

Mollie became pregnant in December 1943 and at the Clinic in Retford she found that Iris too was 'in the Club'. They used to walk to the Clinic together and told us of the refugees who were also attending. From the occupied territories were women of all nationalities, some French, Russian and Polish nationals. We became concerned that news of Mollie's pregnancy would prejudice our chances of retaining our tenancy at the Truswells but we need not have feared, they were most understanding and as excited as we were about the impending birth. We had so much to be thankful for to the Truswells. The 'Second Front'—our assault of the French mainland—was a topic on everybody's lips, and of course Iris was worried that Bert would be involved in the first landings. My position seemed more secure in that there were crews falling over themselves to get to operational squadrons. The Americans were thrusting deeper and deeper into Germany with their daylight sorties and Bomber Command was getting stronger and stronger, their nightly raids keeping the Germans stretched round the clock. There was a prevalent theory that the incessant bombing of German towns and cities would make an invasion unnecessary but this was to prove far from the truth.

I was enjoying life when Mollie had reached the sixth month of her pregnancy. There was feverish activity on the roads, military vehicles of all descriptions were moving southwards and it was evident that the invasion of Europe was imminent.

On 6th June 1944 I was detailed for a cross-country training flight but as I awoke that morning I was conscious of many, many aircraft overhead flying in a southerly direction, and then the radio blared out with the news that our forces had at first light made an assault on the Normandy beaches. Bert had left Ranby camp some days earlier and Iris was extremely worried that he would be among the first to land. It would be several weeks before she heard from him. We hung on every broadcast about the invasion with bated breaths, and could imagine the hell that was breaking loose on those beaches. The gliders and troop-carrying aircraft had our sympathy, we could just see the flak taking out some of those poor souls before they would reach French soil. The radio announced that "All was going well," but knowing from personal experience how tenacious the Germans were I knew that every yard would have to be fought for and casualties would be heavy. All this was going on and here I was still doing cross-country training flights with young men only too anxious to get into the action before it was all over. Standing outside the flight offices one evening, we watched as a Wellington was taking off with a pupil crew going solo for the first time. As the plane took off at the end of the runway, the port engine cut out and the aircraft struggled to gain height. The pilot instructors around me said, "For God's sake, don't turn into the dead engine!" At about 1,000 ft that is exactly what the pupil did and one officer said, "He's had it!" As the Wimpy turned—probably in the hope that he could get on to the end of the runway to land, the plane flipped on to its back and dropped like a stone. There was a thud followed by an explosion and a huge pall of black smoke. Six young men with high hopes would never see their first operation. Other pupil crews waiting to go out for their solo trips were white-faced and shaken. During four years of war I had witnessed so many similar instances but it never became any less distressing.

ELEVEN

Commissioning

Just a week after the D-Day landings I was summoned to the 'B' Flight C.O.—a S/Ldr. S. C. Jolly, and my thoughts were on the possibility of another posting. This was rather perplexing in the light of my living-out plans. It didn't seem possible that I would be posted back to operations again. On entering the C.O.'s office, I was beckoned to a chair and S/Ldr. Jolly ran over my career to date and asked if I had any future ambitions. My reply was that my only plans were to survive the war. He went on to say that with my experience I should have at least achieved by now the position of Signals Leader with the relevant rank. After telling him of my previous interview for possible commissioning and my own reluctance at that time, he said that he was recommending me to attend Group H.Q. at Bawtry for further consideration, emphasising the benefits and advantages of being commissioned. The immediate financial aspects were not attractive, as a Pilot Officer would not be very different to my pay as a Warrant Officer. However, the on-going rewards would of course be beneficial. After further persuasion, I agreed but registered that I would not be greatly disappointed if I was rejected at the interview. The consensus of opinion back at the Sergeants' Mess, discussing it with my instructor friends, was that I should accept a commission if offered so long as it never went to my head and meant that I ignored them thereafter!

So, resplendent in my 'best blue', the transport whipped me off to Bawtry and I entered the old Mansion which housed the Group Headquarters Staff. I felt completely relaxed as I joined five other candidates in the waiting room. The first interviewee, an AC2 wearing a white flash in his forage cap, indicating that he was an aircrew trainee, went in first and reappeared 20 minutes later without any visible signs of how he had fared. A flight-lieutenant then signalled me and opened the door announcing "Warrant Officer Edwin Wheeler D.F.C." At a table sat four uniformed officers of varying ranks and I was addressed initially by an Air Commodore. To his question, "Why did you join the R.A.F. prior to the War?"—I felt that I couldn't truthfully respond with—"Because I wanted a bed!"—so I replied with, "I wanted a career in radio and communications and thought this could be better achieved within the Services." To a question, "Why did you volunteer for Air-Crew duties?" I just had to be truthful and say, "I didn't volunteer, my name together with most of the others on the course was volunteered!" This brought one or two smiles from the interviewing board. There followed a quiz session on my operational career which they found impressive and said so. I think that my speech had improved quite considerably since my previous interview when it had had a distinct Cockney accent, and certainly I had greater confidence. I was not asked any stupid questions as before, such as the Arts, Opera etc., of which I had absolutely no knowledge as I had never had the opportunity. In a very relaxed atmosphere I was informed that I would be recommended for a Commission and was congratulated on my contribution to the R.A.F. in a comparatively short period—five years. I had to wait another couple of hours whilst the other interviewees took their turn before the waiting transport returned to base. There were conflicting views of how the interviews had gone, some chaps having written themselves off completely and others expressing the view that it had been a 'piece of cake'. It appeared that I alone had been told that I was being recommended definitely. I told Mollie the news and she was happy and excited for me. The next step was to await confirmation before going off to Gieves the Tailors for kitting out.

My commissioning was announced in the London Gazette on 25th August 1944 and I was a Pilot Officer in the Reserve of Air Force Officers (R.A.F.R.O.) with a new service number of 56118. The entry into the esteemed R.A.F.R.O. was based on the fact that I had joined as a Regular before the outbreak of war. Although in the lowest commissioned rank of Pilot Officer, my five-figured service number immediately distinguished me as being a pre-war entry and I couldn't be mistaken for a 'rookie' P/O.

My first bank account had been opened at Glyn, Mills to receive my monthly pay and I received my kitting-out allowance which seemed very generous at the time. My pay had risen from 13s/9d (69p) a day as a Warrant Officer to 14s/6d (72½p) a day as P/O but my family allowance increased from 28 shillings (£1.40) a week to 40s/6d (£2.02½) a week. Total resources at about £7 per week might seem insignificant today but I thought I was doing very well just then!

I moved into the Officers' Mess and felt suddenly strange in that no longer could I sprawl in the armchairs as we did in the Sergeants' Mess. We had to observe all the niceties and listen to the boring conversations of senior officers at the bar—where we had to sign for our drinks and pay the mess bill promptly at the end of the month.

Now, of course, in addition to continuing my instructional flying duties, I had to perform various extra duties like Orderly Officer etc. Imagine my embarrassment when entering the Airmens' Mess at lunchtime, listening to the Orderly Sergeant bellowing: "Any complaints?" and being relieved when there were none, but on the odd occasion some bright spark would drum up a trivial complaint just for the hell of it.

On 28th August, Mollie entered Eaton Hall hospital for the birth of our first baby. I remember being very nervous as perhaps most fathers are at this event. Since Mollie's earlier earlier miscarriage I was keeping my fingers crossed that she would not have any further problems.

The next day, 29th August 1944, we were blessed with the birth of a lovely daughter, and I felt so proud and happy that all had gone well. We decided to name her Valerie Anne. When we went back to Ordsall Road, Mr. and Mrs. Truswell welcomed us warmly and treated Valerie as one of their own, fussing over her and making our world complete. We were so delighted with our good fortune, I was determined that we would have another child, hopefully a boy, but that was not all-important, another girl would be equally welcome and would receive all our love.

My flying instructional duties with No. 18 O.T.U. continued through the year without too much excitement except for one incident involving an abortive take-off. Pounding down the runway at about 100 m.p.h., seeing the perimeter track approaching fast and the aircraft still not lifting can be rather perplexing. Tearing through the boundary hedge and finishing in a canal tends to make one think that flying is only for the birds.

TWELVE

Grounded for the Duration

On December 3rd 1944 I made my last flight, just an air test, and by now I had clocked up a total of 1055 hours. The war in Europe was progressing favourably for the Allies, air-crews were coming through in ever-increasing numbers. Tour-expired crews were leaving the operational squadrons and entering the O.T.U.'s for their 'rest' period as intructors. The Adjutant called me to his office and informed me that my flying days were over unless a great calamity occasioned my recall. I was to go to Brackla in the North of Scotland for re-classification. My living-out days were at an end and I wondered where my future now lay. At Brackla I met many aircrew types facing the same problem. The Education Officer gave us a choice of various courses open to us. These included Air Traffic Control, Photographic Interpretation, Controlled Approach Radar, Secretarial or Intelligence, but we would still retain our General Duties (Flying) Status. It was usually a case of 'eeny-meeny-miney-mo'—so many of us were undecided on what course to proceed.

Eventually I opted for radar-controlled approach training but this lasted only two weeks as I found sitting in front of a radar screen talking down aircraft to blind landings was excessively boring. My next choice was joining the P.R.U. (Photographic Reconnaissance Unit) at Benson to undergo training on 'photographic interpretation'. This involved the handling of hundreds of photos, doing line-overlaps etc., identifying and assessing target plots. This needed concentration and enthusiasm and I had neither of these attributes at the time. I almost despaired of ever finding the right niche for my doubtful talents but agreed to try Intelligence. For this I would have to be screened, remembering that I was an 'alias' in the R.A.F. because of my German ancestry, in spite of the fact that I had completed two tours of operational duty against Germany. I found myself posted to the Intelligence Training Unit at Highgate in North London. Just to be back in London was a bonus for me and I could get home to Mollie and Valerie at our flat in Wood Green, less than an hour away, and after attending from 8.30 am to 5 pm daily for training I was free thereafter which pleased me.

The environment at Highgate and the quality of the Training Staff aroused my interest and I was convinced that this was the niche I had been looking for since I had become land-borne. The art of talking confidently to an audience was perhaps the most difficult for me, having never done it before. We were called on to speak on any subject for fifteen minutes which seemed an awfully long time. We had many laughs during these sessions, particularly when we had to respond to awkward questions from the audience. I found the need to research thoroughly before talking on a specific subject. Briefing and interrogation of crews, display of material, liaison with Customs & Excise Officers, Security measures were only some of the areas covered in our training. At the end of the course I was delighted to find that I had been accepted as an Intelligence Officer and anxiously awaiting my posting to a Squadron which I presumed would be within Bomber Command where all my experience had been gained. Imagine my surprise and consternation when I learned that I was being transferred to Coastal Command. My first reaction was that on a Bomber Squadron there was a strong likelihood that I would have known somebody from my days in the Command or at the O.T.U.'s, but in Coastal Command I would know absolutely no one. My request to go to a Bomber Station was refused on the grounds that they were already over-staffed with Intelligence Officers. I had the distinct feeling that my posting would be to an outlandish Coastal base, probably in the Orkneys and was pleasantly surprised when it was announced that I was going to Brawdy in South Wales to a Weather Squadron, No. 517 which was operating in Halifaxes. Looking out of the train window as I passed Tenby on my way to Haverfordwest, I pondered on my future and reflected on the previous five years, and thought how lucky I was to be still around when so many of my friends had gone forever. Transport was awaiting me at Haverfordwest Station for my journey to Brawdy and I couldn't help but feel how quiet it was. Even entering the air base at Brawdy it seemed as if there was no war on, no aircraft were flying and personnel were conspicuous by their absence, nothing like the hustle and bustle one was used to on Bomber Command bases. I felt that I had been put out to grass. Whilst my accommodation was being prepared, I walked into the Officers' Mess which was empty and approached the Bar—a stiff drink seemed to be the solution to all this solitude.

After 30 minutes solitary drinking, three other officers entered the bar and before I could introduce myself, a voice I remembered well shouted, "Bugger me, if it isn't young Eddie Wheeler!" I turned to face an old friend of 1940—it was Charlie 'Chuck' Maderson who volunteered at the outbreak of the war and saw operational experience on Blenheims and Battles. A good-looking Cockney from Battersea in London, Chuck was a happy boisterous type who befriended everybody. For an hour we exchanged conversation on our experiences and I felt so much happier than when I had first entered. Chuck told me that I would find this posting a doddle. Only one aircraft operated in daylight and one at night, flying far out into the Atlantic gathering and reporting weather conditions at zero feet up to 25,000 ft, sometimes landing at the Azores. I asked him if he found that boring but it was apparent that it had many hazards and in fact a number of aircraft had failed to return from such missions. Regardless of the weather, the flights always took place. Finishing our drinking session, I found my spartan accommodation in a pre-fabricated hut but was agreeably surprised to find I had a batman for the first time, and that he would clean my shoes, press my uniform, make my bed and generally look after me, even to tea in bed in the morning. Life was not going to be so bad after all!

My first day began by being introduced to the Operations Staff and of course the C.O. Although there was a Station Intelligence Officer, I was appointed No. 517 Squadron Intelligence Officer and soon made the acquaintance of the aircrews. Wearing the D.F.C. ribbon, I soon found that I was respected by all and sundry and settled down without any ado. My first task was to outfit and update the material in an Intelligence Library regularly frequented by off-duty aircrews. Their main interest was obviously to keep abreast of the progress of the Allied forces in their push eastwards. Things were moving so fast out there that I had all my work cut out to keep the indicated front line up to date. Coastal crews were also constantly interested in U-boat sightings and attacks on shipping. Briefing of the single crews operating by day and by night did not take more than half an hour, so much was repetitive. As Chuck quite rightly said, "It was a doddle."

After two weeks I was not feeling too well as I attended the usual briefing session one evening. I mounted the stage to deliver my latest 'gen' and found myself in a cold sweat with the room going round and round, then I collapsed. Coming round in the sick quarters, the M.O. informed me that I had contracted dysentery and was being shipped to an isolation hospital. I felt so ill I just wanted to die. Arriving at the hospital, a large mansion in extensive grounds, I was horrified to see so many tents with very many patients wandering around in pyjamas and dressing gowns. Being an Officer, I was fortunate to be placed in a room in the main building with six other officers—all suffering from dysentery.

I couldn't fathom out how I came to be infected but it later transpired that it had been contracted from dirty milk. The Station had been drawing milk from a farm without it being pasteurised. I was the first casualty but others were to follow me. I was first given a massive dose of castor oil and every six hours the nurse brought me six M and B tablets—enormous tablets that I had to crunch and endeavour to swallow—mostly without fluid. The treatment seemed drastic but I was told that my stomach lining had to be coated with the M and B to counteract the infection.

The queues for the limited toilets were endless and many suffered agonies and sometimes mishaps when they could wait no longer. Given a small bottle and wooden spoon each morning, we were directed to provide a sample of our stool for analysis. We had to have three successive days of 'negative' analyses but if on two days you had 'negatives' and then a 'positive' on the third day, the treatment of M and B had to be repeated. Many patients had been there for weeks on end and became thoroughly dejected. We waited in the queue for the toilet one morning to provide our sample and everybody became restless and noisy when the occupant had been in there for too long. Nursing orderlies finally came to investigate and when they could not get any response, they decided to break in the door and to their horror found the patient—a German prisoner-of-war—had hanged himself. He had apparently had weeks of getting two 'negatives' and then a 'positive' which had depressed him to the point of eventual suicide. Fortunately I was discharged after only two weeks but I could realise what horrors those wretched prisoners-of-war in Japanese hands had to endure. I was never more pleased to return to Brawdy but I thought constantly about those poor devils queueing up at the toilets with bottle and spoon in hand.

My duties with 517 Squadron didn't exactly stretch me and I had plenty of leisure time to visit Haverfordwest, Tenby and Pembroke Dock. In wartime, these places were not very exciting but any change of scenery was welcome.

When aircraft were returning after having landed in the

Azores, it was my responsibility to advise the Customs & Excise Office at Pembroke Dock of the landing time so that their examining officers could arrive in time to search the plane and crew for contraband or goods on which there was excisable duty. A Senior Officer expressed the view that I was too efficient in advising the Excise Office of the landing times and that perhaps I should gauge my advice so that they arrived ten minutes after the aircraft landed. I considered this to be a test of my honesty and as I had an exemplary record to date, did not wish to implicate myself; furthermore I had nothing personally to gain by acting other than as officially layed down. However, I don't doubt that some crews managed to smuggle some small items, there was too much secret equipment in the aircraft that Excise Officers were not allowed to examine, where watches etc. could be concealed until they left the airfield. It was amazing how, when Mess parties were arranged, training flights were organised to R.A.F. Aldergrove near Belfast in Northern Ireland, and that on their return crates of Guinness were unloaded. On reflection, I suppose we had such few perks in those days that such trips were fair game and generally were given a blind-eye by the top brass.

I had a wonderful relationship with the Operations Room Staff at Brawdy including 'Chick' Henderson—a well known Music Hall performer in better days—who was now an Operations Officer. The Meteorological personnel too were a grand bunch and full of fun. My nostalgia for Bomber Command was fast disappearing, particularly when I read of some of their heavy losses.

The V1 flying bombs and the V2 rockets were causing much concern and I was very worried that Mollie and Valerie were in constant danger back in London at Wood Green. Tragedy almost struck when Mollie was pushing the pram along High Road, Wood Green. Outside one of the big stores she heard a terrific rushing sound and an enormous bang, a V2 rocket had exploded nearby, and the next moment a huge expanse of plate glass shattered and came down over her as she crouched forward to protect

Valerie. Fortunately she was uninjured apart from the shock and she ran all the way home, pushing the pram before her and over the debris, in her words: "In a flat panic." The terrible thing about the V2 rockets was that absolutely no warning was given and they would explode before one was even aware of them. I thought back to Peenemunde and how we had blasted that rocket development base, and now the Germans had developed this horrifying weapon which could cause such devastation and casualties, and could even influence so dramatically the course of the war, in spite of which we appeared now to be winning.

In my capacity as Intelligence Officer, I had access to and was on the circulation list for the Confidential and Secret files, but denied some Top Secret files which I attributed to the fact that I had this 'alias' status throughout my service career because of my German ancestry. This riled me when I thought of the operational service I had rendered to my country and how intensely patriotic I had always been.

One of the most interesting files it was my good fortune to read over and over again was that on U.F.O.'s (Unidentified Flying Objects). The records of sightings over the years, with accompanying photographs, were a complete fascination for me and left me convinced that these 'objects' were authentic and not a figment of the imagination, as so many people would have us believe. It would be interesting to see an updated version of that file now, 40 odd years after World War II.

The war in Europe was going well in our favour, the incessant bombing by the R.A.F. and U.S.A.A.F. against Germany was being maintained with great effect, the Russians were advancing on all fronts, and our push through Italy to the North had gone well; the U-boat threat to our convoys had been overcome and it was just a matter of time before the European conflict was over and we could turn our full resources against the evil Japanese in the Pacific.

With the tempo of life on a Coastal Command Weather

Squadron being such a contrast to the hectic activity on a Bomber Squadron, I had ample time to reflect on what had been an incredible five and more years. So many of my friends, young men, had paid with their lives and there were so many of whom I knew not of their fate and probably would never know. I marvelled at the fact that so many from all walks of life, some from families who only knew poverty and deprivation, had mixed and fought alongside lads from Universities and from very privileged backgrounds. They had discovered a common bond and although there was the usual banter one would expect in such a mixed society, they each respected the other and worked as a close-knit team—war was such a great leveller. Bravery was never confined to one particular type. If only the comradeship and dedication throughout the war years could be carried through to the ensuing peace years, without all the prejudices previously experienced, what a wonderful world it would be.

THIRTEEN

Civvy Street Looming

I pondered on my future when the conflict would be over—should I remain in the Service, or should I take my chances in the dubious world of industry and commerce? Why did I join in the first place? It wasn't for patriotic or romantic reasons, it was basically to get a bed, purely and simply, but what an experience followed getting that bed!

My brother Harry, just a year or so younger than myself, would have no such problem as to what his course of action would be when the war ended. He'd had a bitter experience in the R.A.F. as a member of aircrew.

George, my elder brother, was a Sapper in the Royal Engineers but was never forthcoming about his experiences. A cousin of mine, Kathleen, who was a daughter of my mother's sister Nellie, was a W.A.A.F. based at a Fighter Station at Warmwell in 1941, and recalls April Fool's Day, April 1st, when she watched three aircraft which she believed to be friendly, flying at very low level over the base. So low in fact were the aircraft that she could see the pilots and their goggles, and she gave them a friendly wave. In the next few seconds she was to realise that they were enemy planes as they started machine-gunning and bombing. She threw herself flat on the ground and survived, but ten others were found to be dead when she got to her feet.

The big push towards Berlin, from both East and West,

was going well by March/April 1945 and it was now considered only a matter of time before all resistance was overcome.

Finally, the capitulation of all German forces came on 8th May 1945 and everybody was anxious to celebrate victory with their families or friends. The relief was enormous that the fighting and killing was now over. A day of celebration was announced for May 9th but to my dismay I found that I was Duty Officer that day and would have to remain sober—if ever so slightly. Everybody was congratulating everybody and the bars in the Messes never seemed to want to close. It was one time when I dearly wished that I had been on a Bomber Station. The weather flights still continued as normal and the following few days seemed to be an anti-climax. There were many conjectures as to what would happen in the Far Eastern theatre of the war and how soon the Japanese could be overcome. It was evident that 'Tiger Force' would be supplemented by the more experienced aircrews so that the war in the Far East could be brought to a rapid conclusion. I was informed that my name had been listed for posting to a Lincoln or Lancaster Squadron heading for the Pacific area of operations. I couldn't believe this shattering news but was immensely relieved when I heard that I had been removed from the list on the grounds that my wife was pregnant—and of course there were so many aircrews available and anxious to get in on this final stage of the war.

My mind was made up, I would take the earliest possible release from the R.A.F. and rejoin my family, regardless of the possibilities of my getting suitable employment.

On 6th August 1945 we heard the dramatic announcement that the first atomic bomb had been dropped by an American plane on Hiroshima in Japan, that the bomb had more power than 20,000 tons of T.N.T. and more than 2,000 times the blast power of the British 'Grand Slam' bomb of 22,000 lbs. This was the first time that the World heard of the splitting of the atom. The result of this raid was devastating. A third of the 340,000 inhabitants of Hiroshima had been killed or burned to death and many more thousands were destined to die from the effects of radiation. A second atomic bomb was dropped on Nagasaki three days later with even more appalling results.

The Japanese Government had no alternative but to capitulate within the next four days and V.J. Day (Victory against Japan) was announced on 15th August 1945. The two following days were celebrated as a National Holiday and there were remarkable scenes of rejoicing. After six long years of blackout and gloom, London became transformed into a city of light again and revellers celebrated for three days.

The Japanese signed the declaration of final surrender on 2nd September. Everybody sighed with relief that the ordeal was finally over and that they had survived six horrible years, although almost every family had suffered some grievous loss.

I sat and reflected over the six years, thinking of the very many young men with whom I had the privilege to serve, of the happy-go-lucky friends who had died along the way in their thousands, of the families they had sorrowfully left behind. I thought of them individually, voices and laughter echoing within the crew rooms—I would never forget them, over how ever many years. I wept unashamedly for those wonderful lads when it was all over, the first time I had cried in six years.

What an anti-climax followed. Everybody seemed anxious to rejoin their families and who could blame them? Notice Boards were constantly scanned, all anxious to know their demobilisation release group numbers. Mine was group 26 for release in January 1946. I was asked if I wished to relinquish my opportunity for discharge, being offered a signing-on for a further nine years. I felt it was my duty to rejoin my family, having been blessed with another daughter Barbara on 12th December 1945. Little thought was given to the problem of securing employment or how we would settle down to the hum-drum of civilian life after six dramatic years of war.

Bomber Command was still very busy repatriating troops and P.O.W.'s from all theatres of war, but on a Weather Squadron in Coastal Command all was uncannily quiet until we received orders to proceed to Olympia in London for demobilisation and the issue of civilian clothing.

The big hall at Olympia was a hive of activity. We received our gratuity, £75 in my case, and proceeded to the civilian clothing hall. There were scenes of hysterical laughter as suits, sports jackets, raincoats and hats of varying descriptions were tried on. After six years of nothing but service uniforms, the sight of all these chaps in pork-pie hats, pin stripe suits etc., sent us all into fits of laughter, but finally the N.C.O.'s in charge pushed us out to make way for the stream of buses arriving loaded with 'demobs'. Outside, the spivs were waiting to offer £25 for the complete outfits. Many were happy to take the money and head for the nearest public house with their friends—probably arriving home flat broke.

So, it was all over, and I said to myself: "All that experience—just to get a bed in 1939!"

AFTERMATH

Johnny Sauvage opened his own airline in the Seychelles and eventually became a Director with Thompsons Holidays. 'Hitch' Hitchcock would go back to his job in the bank in London. Denny Denman contracted cancer of the throat and died in Rochford Hospital after the war. Ginger survived to become a Wing Commander and was to become a father of six boys. Tim Yates, a colleague on 214 Squadron and at 27 O.T.U. was to survive to return to his Shropshire farm and become Chairman of Shrewsbury Town Football Club for 25 years. 'Rocky' was finally released from his P.O.W. camp, no thanks to the Russians, and returned to his Kensington home. I returned to work with my pre-war employers, Herbert & Sons Ltd., but after nine months' boredom I applied for re-enlistment in the R.A.F., unsuccessfully. There followed several years in a business set up by myself and my brothers—a garage business in Wood Green, North London but I withdrew to return to Herbert & Sons Ltd. A difference of opinion with their Managing Director saw me off once again, this time to a finance house. Once more I returned to Herbert & Sons Ltd., where I became Company Secretary and Personnel Director until I retired in 1984. Stranger still, the Company moved to Haverhill, Suffolk where I have lived these last 22 years—so close to Stradishall where I started my Wellington operations in 1940. The years have passed so quickly, yet so much has happened over these last five decades. My experience is far from unique, so many of us have stories to tell and should tell them so that future generations are made aware of the life and times of our particular generation, and are able to form their own opinion. I think I owe it to the very many of my wonderful friends and colleagues who died and to those whose lives have been diminished as a result of the war, to write this autobiography.

POSTSCRIPT

Harry Wheeler died on 28th January 1990 before we could publish a joint venture to be entitled "Brothers in Arms".

In his memory I reproduce here a short record of his own war-time experiences dictated by him shortly before his death.

Eddie Wheeler

HARRY'S WAR

I was fortunate to be one of a family of four brothers and two sisters and had the best one could wish for in my mother and father. I loved them all very dearly and hope that a percentage of all the nice aspects in them is somewhere in me.

My story begins in 1940 when World War II was in its infancy, this being the stage in my life when I had to think as an adult, perhaps for the first time, but I found difficulty in adjusting to the fact that I should join one of the armed forces and so take part in events which would lead to a tragic loss of people from all walks of life.

Unlike the youth of today (and are they so wrong?) everybody seemed to be keen to don a uniform and to get into the action to put matters in the world to right.

I chose to join the R.A.F. and confirmation that I had made the right choice was obvious to me when my elder brother Edwin, known always to me as Ted—although throughout his service career he was known as Eddie—came home on leave resplendent in his uniform with brass buttons and badges. I couldn't then wait to follow his pattern and get myself kitted out.

Ted had opted for a Wireless Operator/Air Gunner course and I felt that I was a long way behind him, so I joined the local A.T.C. (Air Training Corps) at Alexandra Palace with a view to becoming a Wireless Operator. I was fascinated with Morse Code and basic wireless and electrics and was soon able to receive and send Morse Code at 12 words per minute which I thought would be beneficial when finally

I entered the Service.

Ted had passed his course and displayed his 'Sparks' badge and to me he could have been an Air Chief Marshal, such was his impression on me! The whole family was so proud of him. I recall his leave because I thought I would capitalise on his expertise as a radio/electrics man, trained by the R.A.F. to wire up an electric light in my bedroom. It would be no problem for AC2 Wheeler, E. R.A.F. No. 647193—or so I thought! In those days we had D.C. current as opposed to our present A.C. current. Ted professionally took a length of wire, stripped the ends and proceeded to divide the strands of wire into two, being the negative and positive connections to the fuse box in the basement and likewise a connection to the socket by my bed. When such an expert was in charge, who was I to suggest that negative and positive should be quite separate and not along the same wire? I was not going to make such a ridiculous suggestion! However, duly connected and quite rightly broken with an on/off switch, we were ready to bow to Ted's superior know-how. Somebody was needed to operate the switch and our lovely young sister, Doris, was duly delegated. I remembered that the air-raid sirens had earlier sounded the 'all clear' when the explosion took place and all the lights went out. Our immediate reaction was: "That was close!" Smoke came up from the basement and on investigation, the fuse box was found swinging from its moorings. My faith in Ted's wiring was not as I had hoped. Ted made his excuses that he had urgently to return to his unit and left us all in darkness. The houses all down the street were also in darkness and this sparked off the investigation by the local Electricity Authority. After the fire subsided, the electrician said that: "The wiring was rotten anyway," and I accepted this to excuse Ted. Mother was informed that proceedings could be taken in view of the unlawful tampering with the Electricity Board's apparatus.

Ted passed his Air Gunner's course and was promoted to Sergeant, rapidly proceeding to O.T.U. (Operational Training Unit). He then went on to a distinguished wartime career that netted him a D.F.C. and Commission after two tours of operations in the European theatre of war.

I was accepted into the R.A.F. to train as a W/OP-A/G and my wireless training at Blackpool and Yatesbury was no problem, my experience with the A.T.C. standing me in good stead. I qualified as a Wireless Operator and was proud to display my 'Sparks' badge. I was then posted to 116 Squadron at Hendon where I gained valuable experience on the key. I also had the opportunity to fly in Lysanders as W/OP, calibrating Ack-Ack and searchlights in the West Country.

Two months elapsed before my posting to Pembrey in Wales for my Air Gunner's Course on Bristol Blenheims. This was my first experience of the cramped conditions in a bomber aircraft. How on earth would I even get into that gun turret and more pointedly, how on earth would I get out in an emergency? The stark reality of being a member of air-crew wasn't so appealing now.

Finally, I passed the Course and became a Sergeant W/OP-A/G and my uniform took on a more glamorous appearance now, but somehow it didn't seem the same as when Ted first appeared after being made up. I seemed to remember my brother being the only one of his kind. When I travelled by train or bus, it seemed that every other person was a W/OP-A/G, AC 'plonks' appeared few and far between.

My next port of call was 15 O.T.U. at Harwell. I saw this as the 'Grand Hotel' where Pilots, Navigators, Bomb Aimers, Wireless Operators and Air Gunners were thrown together for a 'getting to know you' programme. This was where crews were assembled, entirely from your own choosing and not influenced by the establishment. From my point of view, the priority was going to be the skipper (Captain) and so I went looking for an Errol Flynn or James Stewart, but on my first survey all I saw was a Danny La Rue or Franklin Pangbourne (comedy film star of the 40's). Because I was so anxious to be selective and discriminating, most crews had been made up and I was left with little choice. Of the two remaining pilots, one was a 'dead ringer' for Stan Laurel (of Laurel & Hardy fame) and the other a cut-down version of Clark Gable. I chose the latter who turned out to be a Sgt. W. A. Molyneux (Molly) and so I was fixed up and duly introduced to Dave Davison (Navigator), P/O Joe Campbell (Bomb Aimer) and Jimmy Velzian (Rear Gunner). They seemed a great bunch of guys and turned out to be very good at their jobs.

After a week's ground training and classroom work, we started our cross-country flying exercises in daylight on Wellington IC's. We soon found out that the 'Wimpy' was a super aircraft for all crew members, certainly more comfortable than the Blenheim. There was so much more room to move about and with easy access to the 'Elsan' portaloo, which subsequently became a very important piece of equipment as far as our Navigator was concerned.

Our daytime exercises went off quite well with a few bumpy landings but on one occasion we did six 'overshoots' to land in very bad visibility. All and sundry watching down below were laying odds against us getting down at all, and we were very glad to disappoint them, although when we finally touched down we were half way down the runway, failed to stop, went off the end of the runway and what was left of the grass beyond. We then ploughed through a barbed wire perimeter fence, across the main Didcot to Oxford road and straight into another Wellington which also had overshot. Thankfully, we sustained no casualties, but our confidence was shaken.

Night flying was next on the programme and this went quite well. We were adapting to each other's ability, but one snag was that Dave, our Navigator, was very often airsick and spent a lot of time sitting on the Elsan. Our only comfort was that we were assured of a warm seat! His sickness became a major problem as he became almost permanently attached to the 'loo', the Bomb Aimer constantly having to take Astro-shots to get positional fixes. Whilst this could be accommodated during training flights, what would happen when we were operational?

We discussed the problem among ourselves and I personally thought we should make our predicament known to the Flight Commander. The remainder of the crew thought it would be disloyal to Dave and the consensus of opinion was to let the matter ride in the hope that the position would right itself.

Our last night exercise over, a celebration was the order of the day and the WAAFs in the Mess put on a farewell supper for us, consisting of eggs, bacon and fried bread, a rarity, but of course no booze.

Twelve crews were passing out at O.T.U. to join operational squadrons and one of these crews had a problem that came to light before a take-off. The rear-gunner of the crew, named 'Curly' (because he was as 'bald as a badger') was worried about his pilot, Sgt. Ayres (Lew) stating that he had been seen to be drinking double whiskies in the Sergeants' Mess earlier, after learning of his wife's association with another man. When we saw Lew, we too were aware that he had been drinking excessively and the concern of his gunner was shared by us all. Nobody would confront him with the dangers that lay ahead and I failed to understand why it was not reported. Such was the misplaced loyalty of the day, but it was considered disloyal to inform on another crew member and to do so would mean being shunned by the others. We were ushered out to the lorries to take us to the aircraft on the dispersal areas and saw ironically that Sgt. Ayres was due to take off first. I would gamble that 59 pairs of fingers were crossed as he lined up his aircraft on the runway.

The run up of the engines, the green light from control, the release of brakes, then the familiar sound of full power saw him move forward. The roar of the engines got fainter as he sped forward. The navigational lights were clearly visible for what seemed an eternity, but slowly they lifted into the dark sky, banking as they went.

Fingers uncrossed, everybody was happy for 'Curly' and at least his skipper had three hours or so to recover before facing a landing.

We ourselves had a straightforward exercise of three hours or so duration and on returning to base we were briefed to land on a satellite runway at Hampstead Norris. It was a clear night as we approached the circuit prior to landing. We were called by the Control Tower and advised not to land but to join the circuit at Harwell. This became obvious when we saw a Wellington burning fiercely yards short of the runway. No chance of there being survivors, we hadn't kept our fingers crossed long enough for 'Curly' and other members of Sgt. Ayre's crew. I mention this incident as it has a bearing on another that happened much later.

Needless to say, an enquiry into the cause of the crash was opened. "Why had the Pilot been drinking and why on earth wasn't it reported?"—The silent answer—loyalty!!?*!

At this moment in my life I was very fond of a young lady and was sure that she featured very strongly in whatever future I had. I was well aware that my chances of surviving a tour of operations were extremely low and I thought of the forfeit I would be paying in committing myself to the war effort. Nevertheless, my feelings, however strong, would have to be shelved for the duration of the war.

After leaving O.T.U. I was given seven days' leave but during this I was recalled to Harwell where we were to familiarise ourselves with a brand new Wellington being flown in from the Vickers factory—ferried by the tiniest female ferry pilot I had ever seen. Within an hour of its delivery, we were taking off for a few circuits and bumps (landings) and we were delighted with the Mark III's performance.

Things were moving fast now, and we were hauled into the Medical Inspection Room for injections, including one for Yellow Fever. This, we thought, was ominous and subsequently we were briefed to fly this aircraft to the Middle East area of operations within the next few days. With this impending overseas posting, I made a hurried phone call to my girl friend Brenda in Palmers Green which resulted in her arrival next day—chaperoned by her elder sister Eileen. They were introduced to the crew and we had a farewell evening in the Crown Inn at Hampstead Norris Village. Our meeting had been so brief but we said our goodbyes in the right and proper manner.

The following day we flew to Portreath in Cornwall, stayed overnight and then were briefed to fly on to Gibraltar. We all knew what we were leaving behind in the U.K. but had not the slightest idea what was ahead of us.

I recall listening to the B.B.C. who were pumping out the 'Warsaw Concerto' and it seemed to be more like being at the movies instead of going off to war. On the approach to the famous Rock of Gibraltar we were challenged by the aircraft carrier *Illustrious* by Aldis Lamp calling for the appropriate Letters of the Day. As a member of a raw crew, I knew what the reply was to be but couldn't locate our Aldis Lamp to make the response. Time was running short as we made our final approach to land; my first piece of action and I had blown it! So touchy were the Navy, there is no doubt that we would have been prevented from landing if we did not provide the response to their challenge. A quick thought and I loaded the Colours of the Day into the Very pistol and fired it off—praying all would be well. This obviously did the trick and with a sound of applause from all the lads, we were allowed to land.

A few days on the Rock saw our aircraft fitted with extra fuel tanks to enable us to reach Fayed in Egypt.

We had to take a dog-leg course over North Africa due to the fluid position of Montgomery's and Rommel's forces facing up to each other and we were in the air for ten hours.

When we left England, we assumed that we were perhaps only ferrying aircraft to Fayed and would return to U.K. to repeat the operation, after all we had not been issued with tropical kit. However, on delivering the plane, serial number HZ 310, we were promptly advised that crews were a greater priority than aircraft, so what may have been a three-day trip turned out to be the beginning of a three-year term abroad.

We kicked our heels in a transit camp at Heliopolis, Cairo, for a few weeks and so itched to be part of a Squadron—

which we made known to the powers that be. To keep us pacified, we were attached to 216 Group Ferry Command, flying old Wellingtons to Karachi in India, returning each time to Cairo by BOAC Sunderland flying boat. This was quite a pleasant experience until on one particular return trip the flying boat developed problems, making it necessary for us to land on the River Nile at Malakal, south of Khartoum in the Sudan. We were placed overnight in the BOAC Hotel run by a Mr. Sydney Baruch, a pleasant Rumanian who made us so welcome and with whom I was to renew acquaintance in 1945.

Eventually, we were posted among 12 crews to 205 Group Bomber Command being divided between Nos. 70, 37 and 40 Squadrons, and we were attached to the latter.

We went by road from Cairo to an airfield at El Adem, just south of Tobruk, where we joined our Group. There was plenty of activity with daylight and night operations, quite awe-inspiring, and we had our first glimpse of real bombs being trollied around. We were given a few days to settle in and didn't start flying as a crew, our skipper 'Molly' flying as co-pilot and navigator Dave as Second-Navigator with a Canadian, F/O Greenway. For familiarisation, I joined them too as W/Op and Greenway's own W/Op stood down. Our regular gunners were also stood down.

I thought about my first operational flight and felt apprehensive about my ability to cope, thinking perhaps that I should have studied more thoroughly.

My first operation was to be the docks in Pireas in Greece and at briefing I paid particular attention to the location of the radio beacons that would be beneficial on the route. Principally, these were at Cairo West and Habbanijah in Iraq. Whilst I had nagging doubts, I felt confident of being able to take bearings and a running fix, enabling a position plot to be made if the need arose. As it turned out, my main duties on this opening operation were to pour tea for the crew and to throw out an occasional flame float to enable the rear gunner to take a 'wind drift' reading to assist the navigator. The only opposition came from a little light flak, not troublesome, and I must say I was pleasantly disappointed. I thought it would be more traumatic.

The operation was repeated the following night with the same crew but our navigator Dave was due to play his first major role. He had been sick the previous night but the trip was quite straightforward across the Mediterranean. In spite of Dave spending most of his time on the Elsan, we didn't experience any real problems. I constantly took radio bearings in case they were needed urgently. I don't think the skipper even took a course to steer from Dave.

Two trips had been achieved and there had been nothing frightening about them and we classed them as a doddle.

Rommel and his Afrikan Corps were in hasty retreat to Tunis and so our Group moved up to Benghazi.

Our next trip as a crew was to the Docks at Taranto in Italy and it was our first taste of searchlight activity. This operation was more like what we had come to believe night bombing was all about.

Our skipper was, I thought, somewhat ambitious when he decided to do a 'dummy run' over the target. The W/Op position in the 'Wimpy' wasn't exactly the front row of the stalls, very little to see what goes on outside, and one conjured up all sorts of alarming thoughts when evasive action was being employed and the cockpit brightly illuminated by probing searchlights.

The stark white face of Dave climbing over the main spar heading towards the Elsan didn't help the situation. I thought, if only the Captain would hum a little tune over the inter-com to let us know he was happy and in control! We seemed to be over the target area for an eternity.

Eventually, after a life-time, those magic words of John Wayne's—"Let's get out of here"—came over the intercom and to our relief we were heading back to base. By this time, a certain young man on the Elsan appeared to be throwing out at both ends, which made me feel somewhat insecure myself.

Then it happened. The Captain requested a first course to steer on the three-legged track back to base, but it was not forthcoming from the navigator, who had more important things on his mind! The skipper could only guess the first direction to steer—but for how long? Away from the target area, there seemed an awful lot of Italy to starboard.

I took radio bearings from Habbanijah and Cairo but wasn't confident of plotting them myself, so with a map and torch I trundled them down to the unfortunate Dave in his newly appointed 'office' and somehow between us we managed to ascertain a course towards Benghazi. We finally reached the N. African coast but didn't exactly know where. We could get no response to calls on our R.T. (Radio Telephone) so I broke silence on W/T as it was an emergency, sent a signal to Benghazi and asked them to illuminate the Chance Light on the airfield so that we could pinpoint it. Within a short time, our rear gunner spotted it and so we had a visual sighting for home.

Safely down, it was inevitable at the debriefing that we should be asked: "What went wrong?" We were so late on E.T.A. (Estimated Time of Arrival) that we were assumed 'lost'. The skipper said that due to turbulence and violent evasive action, the navigator Dave had become unfit to navigate and when asked if this had happened before, he replied: "No." I wasn't very happy about this but found it too difficult to do anything about it in view of the rest of the crew's attitude. I thought of poor old 'Curly' at O.T.U. He had died because nobody would inform on his pilot, what a price to pay!

With the navigational problems we were experiencing, I realised the importance of my own job and so made a point of spending a lot of time in the ground signals cabin to digest more about my job than the normal training had given me. We had emergency transmitters installed in the aircraft that one could use if the need arose. Devices could be set up for the pilot to steer towards beacons with pin-point accuracy and a number of aids only sketchily touched upon at training school.

After a few weeks elapsed, we were moved up behind the

8th Army at Tunis, being based at an airstrip named Kairoun. The 15th U.S. Airforce shared the same strip—flying B24 Liberators. They constantly practised low flying in the desert to get a co-ordination perfected in order to bomb the Ploesti Oilfields in Rumania. This they did eventually but with mixed success. During this period, I was absorbing as much technical data on all the available radio aids.

The time arrived when Sicily was to be invaded by the Allies and as the Axis troops evacuated to the mainland via Messina, we started to bomb the Straits of Messina bridgehead. All squadrons of 205 Group were called upon night after night and Sicily was plastered with bombs. We did three successive attacks on this one but the Group's first serious losses had started.

Three of our original 12 crews from O.T.U. were shot down by night fighters. On one of the trips over the Messina beaches, I flew with F/O Greenway, the Canadian skipper with whom I experienced my first operation, my own regular skipper being on stand-down.

This trip was to be the most terrifying experience of my life so far. We had been losing aircraft on these sorties, the German and Italian Searchlight defences making life so difficult, we were told by the skipper in advance that whenever we were 'coned' in searchlights, to grab a firm hold on the framework whilst he took violent evasive action—and of course to utter a prayer! The relatively short trip took us into the brightly illuminated target area with plenty of flak but this was indicative of the absence of night fighters. Photographs of the bridgehead were part of our duties, so accuracy was important and straight and level flying had to be carried out. The first run was relatively smooth, but on the second run they picked us up and hammered us. Remembering the pilot's advice, I grabbed the geodetic frame firmly and prayed. Suddenly, it was as if we had hit a brick wall, there being a sickening shuddering effect and the nose went down sharply. We just dropped out of the sky it seemed, plunging into a blackness that was surely the end. Seconds later it was as if we had dropped into water, the impact was so violent. We had been flying at 12,000 ft so I knew that we couldn't have hit the sea so quickly. It transpired that when we were caught by the defences, the skipper selected full flaps, waited until the aircraft stalled, then pushed the nose down and whipped up the landing flaps which caused us to dive so sharply. How the wings stayed on, I shall never know. The pilot told us we were not to reveal his method of evasive action. I happen to know that the pilot, now a retired Sqdn. Leader Greenway is still alive in Canada. If he ever gets to read this, belatedly I say to him: "You ought to have been bloody ashamed of yourself, but at the same time accept my humble thanks for getting us out!" He might even recall how ill we all were and how he had to fly back on the beacon needles I set up for him on Blida and my handing him a map to choose his own course from Blida to Karouan.

Then a decision was made by Group to send a number of Wellington crews on a conversion course on to B24 Liberators. Our posting was to Lydda in Palestine and after a very pleasant two weeks in a rest camp at Nathanya in Israel, we returned to Lydda airport.

We were just four crews led by skippers—Molyneux, Steele, Ells and Wright, but there were only two aircraft available, 'A' for Apple and 'U' for Uncle. Our first experience of the Liberator was exciting and we clambered all over it, finding that you could get very intimate with it inasmuch as you had total access to the interior including the bomb bays, and could be closely acquainted with the full payload—which was not possible in the Wellington.

They appeared very cumbersome, but the two extra powerful engines seemed to make up for its size.

The gunners were far happier with their larger gun-turrets, the navigator had more room and vision in the nose, pity there was no Elsan in that area! The most comfortable position was reserved for the Wireless Operator, on the flight deck immediately behind the cockpit, with plenty of space. From the radio compartment there was access to the bomb bays via a cat-walk which was no wider than 12 inches. The bomb doors rolled up the sides of the fuselage, revealing an enormous opening for the bombs release. However, there was no way a crew member could walk along the cat-walk wearing a parachute, because the bomb rack carriers extended from the cat-walk to the roof of the aircraft. The pay-load was invariably eight 1,000 lb bombs or mines, dependent on the target. Four bombs were in the forward section and four in the rear, being released electrically by the navigator, but manual releases were also available to be operated by—guess who?—yes, the Wireless Operator! If the electrics malfunctioned and bomb release was to be operated manually, most likely in darkness without a parachute, this became a daunting prospect for me. However, exit in an emergency was so much easier than it had been in the old Wimpy, so we were consoled.

The conversion course was mainly concerning the pilot, the equipment for the rest of us being identical to that we had previously experienced.

The daily routine was to be 'circuits and bumps' with a 'screen' pilot additionally and two wireless operators for radio contact with the Control Tower.

Four crews were undertaking this conversion course and we all knew each other well. One fellow, W/Op Sid Tucker and I were always playing cards as the opportunity arose, and so we were never without a deck of cards and a cribbage board. Another good pal was a W/Op. Sgt. John Hall, nicknamed 'Henry' after the B.B.C. Band Leader. Henry hailed from Wigan, a loveable character who was mad keen on rugby football. His habit was to stuff a towel into his flying helmet, call it the ball and taunt all and sundry, defying them to stop him from getting from one end of the hut to the other. Those of us who survived the war must still be carrying the bruises from those reckless days.

With the only two available aircraft, it was announced that I would be flying first with two pilots and another W/Op, P/O Rosmussen from New Zealand. The second aircraft was to carry two pilots and two W/Operators—including my pal Sid Tucker. Awaiting the call when the aircraft would be pronounced 'Ready', we were playing cards and a reasonable kitty had been built up.

The call came that 'A' for Apple was ready. Henry Hall, who had been watching the game said, "Carry on lads, I'll swap with Wheeler because I want to get away early and then I can visit my brother who is stationed nearby." The 'swap' was mutually and thankfully agreed.

Twenty minutes later, the second aircraft was ready so Sid Tucker and I left the game to do our stint, just routine circuits and landings.

At the airstrip, we watched as our friends in 'A' for Apple made a perfect landing and we commented that the Liberator was so different to the Wimpy in that it made a long low approach and was dragged in on its 'fans', whereas the Wimpy made a much steeper descent.

We were alternating take off's and landings with 'A' Apple. Whilst in the circuit for a landing, the skipper asked me to call the Control Tower to report that a train on the railway line that ran at right angles to the runway had stopped and was making a lot of smoke, obscuring our visual approach. Sid took over the radio to pass on the message whilst I went aft to the beam gun position to get a closer look. I was horrified to see below me one of the unmistakeable tail fins of the other Liberator sticking up out of the pall of smoke. It was immediately apparent that there could be no survivors. Further down the runway a smaller aircraft had crashed. It transpired that a Hurricane fighter plane was making an emergency landing and had collided with the Liberator. My own skipper, Molly, was not aware that I had changed places with Henry Hall and he was quite shocked when I stepped out of the belly of our aircraft. We saw the Hurricane pilot sitting on the side of the runway, smoking a cigarette, being attended by the medics. We thought he had only been badly shaken, but it was revealed that he suffered internal injuries and he died later. In total shock, we returned to the hut, saying very little. I spotted Henry's flying helmet that he had not used because it was only local flying. It was still bulging with the towel inside. I had a terrible guilt feeling, but for Henry's offer to swap duties, he would have been alive and I would have met my Maker! I never really lost that feeling.

The next day saw us on the burial detail and the hearse was a truck with five coffins aboard, somewhat of a luxury really, seeing that most of our unfortunate colleagues were treated to a blanket stitched with bandages. Our crew were all pall-bearers and it seemed ironic that I should take one corner of the coffin bearing my dear friend. They were buried in the Cemetry at Lydda and I believe they remained there.

I have always had the inclination to go back to Lydda and thank an old pal for giving me his life, but I shall never ever forget him.

After a fortnight's training, we returned to our Group at Kairoun and formed No. 178 Squadron, doing a sort of O.T.U. in Tunisia whilst waiting to move to Italy which was being gobbled up by the 8th Army and the American 5th Army. During this period we were stood down to allow the U.K. based Squadrons to operate their 'Shuttle Service' of bombing long range German targets and carrying on to North Africa, then doing a reciprocal bombing trip, landing back in the U.K.

The North African base for this was mainly at Blida, just north of us, and sometimes at Maison Blanche.

It seemed that Lancasters and Halifaxes were everywhere and unbeknown to me my brother Ted had crashed at Blida after raiding Friedrichshaven, he being in one of the three P.F.F. Lancasters on that operation. His crew suffered no serious casualties but he was at Blida for a whole week. If only I had known, I could so easily have made the trip to Blida to see him. We hadn't met for three years and the odds appeared that we would never meet again. Fortunately, this was not the case.

We then moved into Italy, setting in at the very large base at Foggia, dominated by the presence of the U.S. Air Force with seemingly hundreds of Flying Fortresses.

Of the original eight crews I was with at O.T.U. at Harwell, only four now remained—which, I suppose, was a reasonable average. We were soon to lose yet another crew in our first week at Foggia. With only six Liberators, the Squadron started operations to the north, mainly the marshalling yards at Vicensa. We carried only 6,000 lb of bombs because the four Pratt & Witney engines could not match the performance of the two Hercules Mk 3 engines of the Wellington.

This being the case, my old card-playing partner Sid, had a first-class pilot named F/Sgt. Ells and complained that his aircraft was underpowered and that he had doubts about there being sufficient runway to lift off with 6,000 lb of bombs. The Commanding Officer, Wing Commander Dickie Smythe, was recognized as a hard taskmaster who rather belittled F/Sgt. Ells by testing his aircraft with 4,000 lb of bombs, lifting off just two-thirds of the way down the runway, assessing that the other third would adequately lift off the extra 2,000 lb of bombs.

So it was that F/Sgt. Ells, Sid, and crew started their run with 6,000 lb of bombs. We all watched with fingers crossed. Every inch of the runway was used and at the perimeter, the pilot pulled her up but the rate of climb was painfully slow. We never saw that crew again, there was no Mayday distress call and no communication was forthcoming. We all developed a healthy hatred for old Dickie Smythe thereafter.

At this stage, we said farewell to Dave, our navigator, who was posted back to 40 Squadron and quite frankly I had a sense of relief. He was replaced by a Canadian, Flying Officer Woods.

With just four operational aircraft we took on a different role. Nuisance bombing became the name of the game and we worked in conjunction with the Yanks. Marshalling yards to the north and dock areas were our targets. We operated in pairs, one aircraft running in to the target area would drop the bombs singly whilst the other would orbit and drop bundles of 'window'—tin-foil strips that would play havoc with the Radar below, thus confusing searchlight and flak units. This would go on throughout the night hours, very boring for us, but we had little opposition to worry about. The Yanks would take over throughout the hours of daylight with their pattern bombing. The idea was to prevent or disrupt the unloading of supplies from trains or ships. This procedure became a regular chore, just like a bus route.

On one occasion, Genoa was the focus of our attention for 'nuisance' bombing. Six runs over the target were timed to perfection. To offset our boredom, at around 21.30 hours I picked up a B.B.C. broadcast on my Marconi receiver and we had a sing-along with Anne Shelton. All seemed to be going smoothly but complacency made me miss the half-hourly broadcast from base—this being an immediate recall of all aircraft to base. We all had the feeling that light flak at 11,000 ft was nothing to worry about. Don't believe it! A direct hit amidships shook us rigid. An almighty bang, with showers of sparks etc. through the bomb-bays, promptly put paid to our sing-along.

The skipper brought us out over the Mediterranean with no apparent malfunction of the plane and I went aft to assess the damage. On either side of the top main spar was a gaping great hole. Apparently the A.A. shell found the oxygen bottles which duly exploded and took out quite a lump of fuselage. Our gyro compass was also affected. I went to the flight deck to report the damage and all seemed to be well, except that our compasses gave different readings. No coastline was visible. Not knowing the possible consequence of events, we decided to transmit an emergency signal on our I.F.F. transmitter. This was a transmitter to provide identification between friend or foe but it also had an automatic S.O.S. signal built-in.

We still had four 1000 lb bombs on board, so the navigator made them 'safe' and jettisoned all four together. Whilst I was trying to aid the pilot by setting up a homing procedure on a radio beacon at Bari in Southern Italy, we were joined by a Bristol Beaufighter off our starboard wing tip. To see this aircraft suddenly loom up initially frightened the life out of us but he took immediate evasive action. Then we realised that possibly this was our 'ticket home'. Unable to establish R/T contact with the Beaufighter who no doubt could see our damage, we followed him, but with great difficulty. We slowly descended until eventually we sighted the volcanic islands of Stromboli ahead and with a calculated turn to starboard, it was not long before we sighted Foggia which had been specially illuminated for us by the Chance Lights. We landed safely to be greeted by some ten anxious people.

Some three or four months elapsed before we were given leave, and this took us to Rome and the Vatican. At St. Peter's Church we were met by an Irish Priest and before long we had an audience with Pope Pious. The priest volunteered to show us around the Vatican and in the course of conversation, our skipper said how wonderful it was that both opposing sides in the conflict had agreed to spare Rome from bombardment and make it an open city. The priest concurred but said "In fact, bombs did fall into the Vatican City, but failed to explode." His belief was that this was done purposely by one side to discredit the other, creating the impression that the agreement to spare Rome had been broken.

Later on we were struck by the thought—"Could these bombs to which the Priest had referred have been the ones which we jettisoned 'safe' in the emergency?"

On our next trip to the Vatican, we could not locate our Irish Priest but approached another one, with a view to making discreet inquiries of the said bombs. He volunteered the information that two unexploded bombs had been found in the Vatican but would not divulge their size, make, or even when they were dropped. Studying the map of Italy, Genoa, Rome and Stromboli are virtually in line and the time of jettisoning could be assessed as it would take a Liberator about one hour to fly from Genoa to Rome. Our minds boggled at the thought that we could be responsible for this incident, but if only two bombs were found, were there still two others waiting to be found?

It was now Spring of 1944, the Allies were driving ahead well north of Rome and our operations were becoming spasmodic. The U.S. Air Force was still doing its daily chores, but there seemed little for our three remaining Libs to do. That is, until some bright spark thought we could be usefully employed laying mines in the River Danube. Prior to starting on this new venture, we fitted in a few trips over Yugoslavia, not with our usual hardware but with Navy and Army personnel complete with radio equipment. Strange to see these poor guys going out of the bomb bays instead of our usual bangers. We thought, "This is a doddle, just suit us till the end of hostilities," until returning to base after one of these sorties, we found that we had lost yet another crew. Subsequently, we were told that the crew had all baled out, but their skipper, Captain Blake, a South African, had been shot by his captors—purportedly trying an heroic escape. The theme of 'Ten Little Nigger Boys' kept going through our minds.

However, two more clapped-out Liberators joined us to bring our strength up to four and then we started our trips to various stretches of the Danube.

We carried four 1,000 lb mines, fitted with parachutes to slow their entry into the water. They were magnetic in operation to detonate when shipping came into the near vicinity. It seemed that the surrounding terrain to the Danube was somewhat hilly and as we were directed to drop the mines from only 1000 ft this was decidedly 'dodgy' unless we had the benefit of moonlight. One consolation was that there was no ground activity or interference from any source. Nevertheless, in view of our previous experiences, we were all decidedly on edge. Even the skipper, a dedicated man to his job, would sweat profusely prior to take-off. I had always been concerned for the welfare of the other crew members and made a point of studying their duties and attitudes. For example, the Mid-upper Gunner was located in his turret immediately above the Wireless

Operator's position and he was completely mobile including his oxygen supply. I made it my duty to keep his oxygen supply topped up from the main source. I was aware when he was running low on oxygen because the regular rotation of his turret would cease and he would drift into a pleasant sleep. O.K. for him, but this would constitute a danger to the rest of us as a fighter attack could be over within seconds. Hardly a round of ammunition was ever fired by our gunners, other than when they were testing them. So, this task became boring and tiresome, making them too relaxed and lethargic, unlike the experience of the gunners in the European theatre of operations who were faced with the prospect of constant attacks by night-fighters.

To get over the problem of sleeping or dozy gunners, I enlisted the help of the ground crew and persuaded them to drill a hole in the perspex, the purpose being to allow the inlet of a draught of air. This did the trick for a while until the resourceful Jimmy Velzian, hailing from the Orkneys, used a well-chewed piece of gum to plug the hole in the perspex, so we were back to square one!

My crew position was immediately behind the cockpit, no bulkhead door separating us. Prior to take-off I would mentally go through the cockpit drill with the pilot, a routine that was of paramount importance to safety.

On our first mine-laying operation, we wondered how this could possibly help the campaign but then reckoned that the mines were surplus to requirements and this was the best way to dispose of them.

The skipper went through his cockpit drill and I watched closely. He made his selections of mixture, flaps etc. and through to 'cowgills closed'. This procedure referred to the segments at the back of the engines and these would normally be opened whilst on the ground or taxiing etc. to prevent the engines overheating. However, on take-off it was essential for the cowgills to be 'closed' as otherwise they would act as a brake and seriously affect the take-off.

Cockpit drill completed, we started our run down the

runway and I sat down and braced myself. Suddenly I realised that I hadn't seen the pilot operate the closing of the cowgills although he had voiced it as part of his cockpit drill. I quickly jumped up to a small window on the flight deck, overlooking the main plane, and to my horror saw that the gills were all fully open. Rushing back to the cockpit, having no time to switch on my inter-com, I lifted the pilot's earpiece and shouted "Cowgills." We were a quarter of the way down the runway so had ample time to abort the take-off. The pilot informed Control that he was concerned about an engine noise, no reference to the cowgills, of course. Molly, the pilot, gave me a full dressing-down for interfering and this I failed to understand. What might have happened if we had carried on? My mind boggled as we made our grand second run which was satisfactory. On arrival at the dropping zone, we found it virtually impossible to get to the directed height of 1000 ft on a stretch of water that snaked through high ground surrounding it. Two attempts were made before deciding to abort. How many times have aircrews said, "Sod it, let's drop them anyway and get out of here?" Molly wouldn't do that and decided to look for another suitable stretch. This kept us over the target area twice as long as was allowed for. The remainder of the crew were unanimous that we should get out, but the skipper insisted on trying again and again. Finally, we did drop the mines but none fell into water, a wasted effort!

I decided it was a bit late in the war to become an Errol Flynn and was increasingly agitated with all that seemed to be happening. I was convinced that the odds were shortening against us.

We lost yet another aircraft during these operations and this lessened confidence even further. I felt already that I had been living on borrowed time since the accident in Lydda, and what was happening now seemed to be so futile.

The Wellington Squadrons in the Group were also mine-laying now. Nobody was 'hogging' trips now. 'Hogging' meant that any crew member, other than the pilot, could volunteer to take the place of members in another crew, in order to complete the requisite 40 operations to finish a tour and thus enjoy a well-earned rest from flying.

The war in Europe was going very well for the Allies now and it was just a matter of time, but the end of hostilities was in sight.

We had a quiet period for a while as we went from 1944 to 1945. The weather improved and we were back into minelaying again.

At that time, if we had flown the previous night, it was highly unlikely that we would be called again to fly the following night.

Sergeant Birkbeck, a friend who was not attached to any particular crew, in fact a spare 'bod' in the pool of aircrew, managed to get two tickets for a show the Yanks were putting on in Foggia. It was suggested that we get into Foggia early, have a meal, go to the American bathhouse to freshen up and then on to the show. But firstly, it was necessary to go to S.H.Q. to establish who, if anybody, was on flying detail that night. These flying orders were put into a clip-board and displayed on the Crew Notice-Board. A quick glance told us that we were not among the crews selected which seemed in order as we had flown the night before.

We duly signed out at the Guard-house and grabbed a lift into Foggia. A good evening was enjoyed, after which we returned to base.

On signing in we were immediately placed under open arrest for apparently being absent without leave (AWOL). We thought this was crazy! We were informed that we had both been detailed to fly that night but there had been a delay in take-off times.

The fact that we were not at briefing would have provided plenty of time to obtain replacements from the aircrew pool of spare bods.

The recurring problem of 'keeping mum' about crew members came up again—my skipper had said nothing, but hoped I would get back in time to fly. His so-called 'loyalty' did me no favours, the problem would never have arisen had he declared that I was not available and in such circumstances another standby Wireless Operator could have been allocated. As it was, at the last minute, the C.O.'s bosom pal, Squadron Leader Wells, the Navigational Officer, stepped into the breach as my replacement and of course this led to a Court of Enquiry.

Subsequently, I was to appear before the C.O. to answer the charges of AWOL. Prior to going in to the C.O.'s office, I was briefed by Warrant Officer Paddy Kelly, who was a fatherly figure, well respected by all aircrew members.

Taking me to one side, he said that I would be formally charged and that I would be given the option of accepting the C.O.'s punishment or alternatively going before a Court of Enquiry. It was generally the practice to accept the C.O.'s punishment, but W/O Kelly expressed the view that I should opt for the Court of Enquiry which would take some considerable time to come about—during which time I would be grounded. I was given 30 minutes to make my decision. My skipper, 'Molly', was at hand and I asked for his advice. He replied that the decision had to be mine but added, "If I were in your position, I know what choice would be obvious to me!" Flying had become so hazardous, his comment convinced me to opt for the Court of Enquiry, so I had made my decision.

I was grounded pending the outcome of the enquiry which, I was informed, was to be held in Naples on a date to be advised.

My defence would be that I could see no listing of our crew for flying detail on the night in question. Rumour had it that someone unknown had removed the said notice to the Mess to study it, but this was not substantiated.

Early the following morning, I was awakened by a Pilot, F/Sergeant Les Steele, with the news that 'Molly' and my old crew had failed to return from a raid on Bucharest. I was stunned but frankly not surprised. I had the same awful feeling I had when Henry Hall had taken my place in Lydda and was killed. Who said that fate plays a hand in who should live or die? Les Steele was the sole surviving skipper from the eight who had left Harwell O.T.U. together.

I was duly posted to Naples, where in a transit camp I had time to reflect on all that happened over those months in North Africa and Italy. The only consolation I had was that a certain young lady was waiting for me back home and until now I didn't think I would ever see her again. But now I had something to hold on to and look forward to.

I was placed in a Services Canteen for a while, to supervise its operations—just for something to occupy my time and to alleviate the boredom. Eventually I was summoned to S.H.Q. to be informed that I had been tried at the Court of Enquiry and found 'guilty'. I was not even allowed to attend the Court to present my defence. The outcome was that I was stripped of my stripes, downgraded to L.A.C. (Leading Aircaftsman), and posted to Africa—a Staging Post 200 miles south of Khartoum in the Sudan. I had no rights of appeal against the Court's decision.

I weighed up all the pros and cons and came to the conclusion that being alive compensated for all the bad things that had happened.

Constant memories of Molly, Jimmy, Ken, Harry and Henry Hall are, and always will be, etched on my mind to the end of my days. I think also of W/O Paddy Kelly who counselled me at a time when I was prepared to walk the other way, so—"Thank you, Paddy!"

No. 28 Staging Post was a lonely airstrip called Malakal on the River Nile and this was where I was to spend my last five months in the R.A.F. I was put into the Transmitter & Receiver Radio Station to maintain contact with the Dakota aircraft ferrying from Italy to South Africa, mainly taking South African service personnel home.

The war was now over in Europe and I had survived where so many others had perished.

I heard that my brother Ted had made it against overwhelming odds and I was so delighted that the Wheelers had come through. My delight was blunted when I received the "My Dear Harry" letter from Palmers Green telling me that what I had been looking forward to for so long was not to be. Three and a half years was, I suppose, a very long time for anybody to wait, but I slowly began to understand what the war had done to us. I was getting older now, in fact I was 23, but felt I had lived a lifetime in a comparative short number of years.

Malakal was, perhaps, the best place to recuperate, our duties were minimal, discipline was not tight and we had plenty of time to appreciate the wonderful wild life in the area.

However, 'ere long, I was caught up by a bloody mosquito that knocked me out with two types of malaria. I was convinced that I was going to die and that this was some sort of retribution for what had gone before. It was very nearly the end until a South African doctor was flown in from Khartoum to give me a lumbar puncture which, eventually, broke the fever and I slowly recovered.

The lads in our group were a super bunch and they laid on a party to celebrate my recovery. They booked into the local B.O.A.C. Hotel to which crews from Sunderland Flying Boats would go after landing on the River Nile.

Earlier, I mentioned that when we were attached to 216 Ferry Command, ferrying Wellington ICs to Karachi in India, we used to come back by B.O.A.C. flying boats and land near Malakal. It was there that I met the Manager of the Hotel, a Rumanian named Sidney Baruch, totally pro-British and who loved the R.A.F. It was my pleasure to meet him again at this party and he did us really proud. He supplied all our food and service at his own expense, while we paid for the booze.

During the meal, we heard that a Sunderland had made an unscheduled stop and a few passengers had disembarked to stay at the hotel. Of these, one turned out to be the Agha Khan together with his wife, the Begum. Apparently, he had felt uncomfortable and decided to break his journey at Malakal and stay overnight. He joined us at our table and when he learned of the purpose of our celebration, he settled our bills for us. It was a very pleasant experience. He returned shortly after and we remained in the lounge with Sidney Baruch, who insisted that we all keep singing *Land of Hope and Glory,* which we did until the tears ran down his cheeks.

1946 came, time for me to be demobilised, but until this day I feel that the whole mantle of my life was spent in the war years. My best friends, and family, are very dear to me and will always be so. I particularly remember the very young men I was privileged to be associated with, and feel a sadness that the circumstances that befell me never came their way. I believe many of them would have welcomed such opportunities—especially when I recall my old skipper Molly saying—"Harry, the choice is yours, but I wish I was in your situation to make such a choice."

I say now to all surviving members of Aircrew, your experiences must all have been similar to mine, and those memories will be engraved on your minds for the rest of your days. Rightly so, because you and the families of lost ones will only remember those lads as they really were—super guys who are as real today as they were then.

I truly hope that they did not give their lives in vain.

"We will remember them."

Dictated by Harry Wheeler, ex R.A.F. on 5th November 1989.